WAR FOR WHAT

by

Francis W. Springer

Publisher
Bill Coats Ltd.
1406 Grandview Dr.
Nashville, Tennessee 37215

WHAT WAS THE REAL CAUSE OF THE WAR BETWEEN THE STATES?

One must understand the events that preceded it, and to understand those events, one must look further back, and back again, until some reasonable starting point is reached.

At what point should we start? Causes started building up before the English landed on Jamestown Island in 1607. The activities of the Portugese and Spanish in their vigorous exploitation of Columbus' Discovery had important bearing on all events here from then on.

This discussion brings out some of the significant events that followed. Many will be familiar enough, but others, seldom if ever publicized, may not.

Francis W. Springer

ISBN 0-931709-02-4 5.95

CONTENT

I   VIRGINIA'S ONE-CROP ECONOMY   1
Who set the world on fire? With what? Who were
slaves? To what. Why didn't the English stay
home? Others did. What did they really want?
Strange paradox.

II JOB OPPORTUNITIES   6
A short life but not a merry one. With a labor
surplus in England, why import Africans? Why
slaves? Who was "Father of African slavery" in
Virginia?

II SLAVES OF TOBACCO   12
Why only tobacco? ALL necessities could be
grown in Virginia. Some figures and facts, costs
and computations.

IV WHAT NOBODY KNEW   18
A few knew. Why not all? How much do WE
know of OUR future? Even of our past? Slavery
and history.

V   AFRICA'S ONE-CROP ECONOMY   22
Who raised the crop: Who harvested it? What
did Africa import? What did Africa do with the
profits?

VI MIDDLE PASSAGE   27
Why target THIS? The horror trip? What alternative?

VII DISPLACED PERSONS   31
Who displaced them? Send them back? Did they
want to go? COULD they go?

VIII ABOLITIONISM 35
What was it trying to do? How? What did it do?
How many were freed? Another one-crop economy.

IX BEHIND THE FAN 48
Facts and figures fault favorite fallacies

X COMPROMISES AND CONCESSIONS 52
The beautiful balance bulges. Who was the most
far-sighted man at the Constitutional Convention?

XI ENCIRCLEMENT 55
A circle that couldn't expand. Another one-crop
economy. Why not slaves for that?

XII LOP-SIDED LEGISLATION 60
How good is majority rule? The arithmetic of freedom. Capital and Labor?

XIII WAR CLIMATE 66
The "Age of Invective". Climate or climax? The
"Gilded Potomac".

XIV THE FIRST SHOT 70
Union AND liberty? Union OR liberty? Who
wanted war? Who wanted peace? Who refused to
strive for peace? A moment for statesmanship.
The first act of war.

XV EXCITING ATMOSPHERE 81
Odds with no ends. Mistakes in arithmetic. Their
native health.

XVI   EVERYBODY WORKS   90
"Sciences" of war. War makes work but who's to
do it? Logistics and statistics.

XVII HOW MANY MEN?   95
Awesome odds. More arithmetic. How big an
army? How big a population?

XVIII TO WORK OR FIGHT?   102
How do both? Which is more important?

XIX   CONTRABANDS   107
Freedom means what? Out of the frying pan?

XX   THE PROCLAMATION   110
What was it supposed to do? What did it do?
What about the Constitution? The Crittendon
Resolutions?

XXI   OVERDRAFTS   113
Re-used heroes. Involuntary volunteers. Too
much liberation.

XXII PSYCHOLOGICAL WARFARE   119
Kind hearts are more than bayonets. Vandalism. What is prejudice?

XXIII END AND BEGINNING   124
Which gun made the most noise? The arithmetic of attrition.

XXIV A WAR BY ANY OTHER NAME   130
Would a better name make a better war?

XXV   LEGALISMS   134
       When is a constitution not a constitution? When
       is a state not a state? Cards face up. Unsolved
       who-done-it.

XXVI   THE DESPOT'S HEEL   149
       On whose neck hardest? An awakening from a
       dream. Liberation from the liberators.

XXVII WHAT IF IT HAD MIS-FIRED?   157
       They often did. Who would have done what? A
       monkey wrench in the political machinery.

XXVIII THE LIBERATORS LEAVE   161
       What did they leave? Is fratricide justified? An
       enormous blunder. A stained glass window and a
       political speech.

XXIX   TECHNOLOGY AND SOCIOLOGY   168
       Some still visible results. What could have been
       but for what?

XXX   BEYOND THE CALL OF DUTY   172

       ACKNOWLEDGEMENTS   185

       REFERENCES   186

       POPULATION CHARTS   200

       INDEX   208

       BIBLIOGRAPHY   212

       ADDENDA   214

CHAPTER ONE

VIRGINIA'S ONE-CROP ECONOMY

Although the Pilgrim Fathers seem to get most of the publicity here and abroad, the first English settlement on the North American mainland was established at Jamestown, Virginia in 1607.

By the time the first Yankees-to-be landed on Plymouth Rock, Virginians had made a lot of history. Virginia's House of Burgesses, first representative governing body in the New World was functioning. Virginia's tobacco industry had been launched into vigorous competition with Spain with a product comparable in quality with Spanish tobacco. The first Negro workers for Virginia's tobacco fields had landed on her shores and Virginia was the home of a live population that probably exceeded one thousand white people and the graveyard of four times that number.

It is seldom mentioned that this effort was the fourth attempt by white people to settle in the mid-Atlantic section of what we know as the United States. The first try was made 83 years before, when 600 people, including some Negro slaves set sail in 1524 from Santo Domingo for a point near the Jamestown site. After a disastrous year, only 150 survivors, with one ship, made it back to home port. Again in 1570, an expedition of armed Spanish Jesuit missionaries, unaccompanied by soldiers, was massacred at about the same location; and it was not far from there that Sir Walter Raleigh's Roanoke Island colony disappeared in 1585, giving history one of its most intriguing mysteries.[1]

The 1607 colony came near being just another failure. At the end of its first two-and-a-half years there were 500 colonists still alive there but by the end of that year only 60 survivors of disease, starvation, accidents and arrows were but half alive when Lord Delaware showed up with fresh supplies and personnel. By 1622, after the colony had been in existence fifteen years, and somewhere near 5,000 men and women had shipped out from England and sailed

★ERROR: Paragraph 3, Line 8
Again in 1570, an expedition of unarmed

up the James toward a new future, there were only 1240 still alive; but in March of that year, a sudden, well planned attack by the Indians killed 347 of them. But the stream of immigrants never slackened.[2]

The Spanish, with strong outposts in the West Indies and at St. Augustine, claimed the entire continent and regarded the English as trespassers. More than once, Spanish spies reported that the English colony was weak and could easily be destroyed; but in view of previous experience, the Spanish king believed that Jamestown could not be successfully colonized, and he sought to punish any of his people who advocated colonization in that area. He was sure that the English were wasting their money and would shortly go broke there; but there were two things the Spanish didn't know. They didn't know that tobacco would soon be worth more than all their gold and jewels, and they did not know that good tobacco could be grown in Virginia. Who could predict such things?[1]

Spanish and English objectives were different. Religious fervor was a major motive of the Spanish kings and missionary clergy who thought that their heavenly estate would be greatly improved if they could convert the New World to Christianity, and that eternal salvation would be vouchsafed any king who could bring England back into the fold. Their expeditions to the Americas always included a number of padres, many of whom endured unimaginable hardships and tortures in their zeal to bring the Word to the savages. It was not their fault that they also made straight the way for the seekers after gold, the traders in furs, and the conquistadors ambitious for new domain.

Rivalry between the two great nations of Spain and England accounts for most of 17th century history. Amazingly energetic, the Spanish were first on the scene and the extent of their explorations into the unknown and hostile American hemisphere shows what formidable opponents they were; but it was treasure that ruined Spanish hopes. Gold, silver and jewels are not in themselves of great economic value. With all the wealth that they brought back from the New

World, the Spanish failed to build a healthy economy. They did not even provide an adequate navy or merchant marine for the safe transportation of their riches, and were liberally plundered by tough English privateers like Drake, Hawkins, Morgan and others. The attitude of Spain toward Virginia was the result of the king's unsound policy. He knew that there was no gold or silver there and had no incentive to undertake an expensive expedition to push the English out and set up an outpost of his own. He kept Jamestown under surveilance but made no effort to attack it.

The English, on the other hand, were not primarily concerned with treasure. They did not disdain gold and silver, and had some hope of finding both in Virginia, reasoning that if Indians to the south possessed such immense wealth, those to the north must also have some too. Although many people still have the notion that the early Jamestown settlers were "indolent aristocrats" who brought their servants here to pick up gold nuggets lying around so they could return to a life of luxury in England, it has been pointed out often enough that England was more in need of such everyday things as potash, soap ashes, iron, copper, wine, silk, hemp, cordage, pitch, dyes, tar, turpentine, glass and, most prosaic of all—wood. Wood for building ships, houses, barns, wagons and a thousand other useful articles, and for making charcoal, the only fuel that could produce fire hot enough for smelting iron and fashioning metals.

But wood did not fire the popular imagination. It was tobacco. That one word shook up the whole world. Everyone, it seemed, was taken suddenly tobacco crazy. The insatiable demand for this new herb wrote the script, cast the characters and set the stage for a drama of which the last act has yet to be performed. People everywhere, then and since, have been willing at whatever sacrifice, to part with their money for tobacco and in Virginia for 150 years, tobacco WAS money. Even clergymen were paid in tobacco, and one clergyman brought suit when his vestry insisted on paying him in coin of the realm.[1]

But Spain was in control of the world's tobacco supply.

Their West Indian plantations were furnishing the world. England itself was buying thousands of pounds, and King James I was trying to discourage what he called "the filthy habit of taking tobacco". (Virginia tobacco was then too harsh for the world market.)

Virginia tried to grow other crops and export other commodities, with no great success, and there was little to brighten the prospects of the colony until John Rolfe, husband of Pocahontas, developed a better curing process and also bought (or stole) some seeds of the Spanish West Indian variety. He produced an experimental crop on Sherley Plantation 20 miles below what is now Richmond. When the first shipload of this new tobacco reached England in 1613, it met with immediate acceptance. It proved that the same choice product could be raised in Virginia as in the West Indies, and from that moment Virginians became slaves of a one-crop economy. King James then saw the futility of opposing the use of tobacco and saw the profitability of slapping a tax on it.

Everything in Virginia became dependent on the tobacco crop, and there was no use in trying to produce anything else. All other crops failed the test of profitability. Tobacco failed too sometimes, but good times followed bad, and tobacco kept Virginia in business and enabled the English to win their struggle for existence against Spanish aspirations. Nothing else could have saved Virginia.

It is one of the great paradoxes of history that the Indian gave white men tobacco which enriched them, while the white man gave the Indians whiskey which destroyed them. Strange is it not, that tobacco did not enrich the Indians, and that whiskey did not destroy the white men (or hasn't yet). Stranger still, our federal government which, half a century ago thought that whiskey would destroy us all, now thinks that tobacco will do it; but perhaps not so strange, many drinkers of whiskey and smokers of tobacco think that the federal government will be our destruction.

But the 17th century was a time for action, not for idle reflection. The expanding British population, in a life-or-death struggle with Spain for existence as an independent nation, made it imperative that they establish and at all costs safeguard supply lines of the commodities needed for subsistence.

(Morgan, pp.180-195) Berkeley had plans for diversification but English capital was not available for industries other than tobacco; so capital for other ventures would have to come from Virginia, actually from tobacco. That would be using the tobacco industry for the purpose of crippling it and that wouldn't work. It would be taking capital created by a profitable industry and investing it in a less profitable, probably unprofitable, one.

CHAPTER TWO
JOB OPPORTUNITIES

Lives were short in the early years of Virginia, too short for most of the colonists to realize the dreams that had brought them in tiny ships across a stormy ocean to a savage wilderness. The Tidewater section was low, swampy and hot. There were mosquitoes and malaria, contaminated water and dysentery. Three-fourths of those who came to Virginia to carve out for themselves a bright new future did not survive the second summer. They came as novices without experience and didn't live long enough to acquire any. Virginia was full of neophytes. Seventy-five percent of the people who were trying to build a new country, solve the problem of creating a new economy and make long range plans, had no knowledge or experience on which to draw.[1]

There was no book of rules, and few knowledgeable people for the newcomers to consult. Indians taught the white man how to raise tobacco and other products peculiar to this land that was so new to the English and Europeans, but the Indians wouldn't raise tobacco for the white man. They did not like the white man's way of life which required that the men, not the squaws, do the drudgery in the fields. Raising tobacco demanded the work of many hands, and most of the operations required a minimum amount of skill. In addition to knowledge and experience, the white people needed a great deal of unskilled and semi-skilled labor.

From the first, English colonial planters imported "indentured servants" from England. Indentured servants were not housemaids with false teeth. They were not servants at all in the modern sense. They came from many classes. They were craftsmen, farmers, adventurers, gentlemen, even some younger sons of the nobility who signed up to work for a period of time and thus get started on a career as independent planters themselves. It was a simple system and effective for a time. When a planter built up some credits in England, he would arrange for his financial representative to pay the passage of a young man in return for an agreement to work for a period, usually running from three to seven years. The planter would be granted 50 acres for each worker he imported, and the worker would also be granted 50 acres upon completion of his contract of service. (Some say that there were more 50 acre grants than there were indentured servants imported but that is beside the point.)

The point is that, with such a high mortality rate, many indentured servants did not live to complete their indentures, and the system became an extremely expensive means of securing labor for the tobacco fields. Besides, these "go now, pay later" people never worked for wages after completing their contracts. Those who survived the hazards of sunstroke, disease or a tomahawk in the back of the skull, became independent planters immediately upon their discharge. Some ran out on their contracts but defectors were usually sent after and if found were dragged back and made to serve additional time. Men convicted of crimes, including the "crime" of being in debt, were often sentenced to "slavery" for a period of years in the colonies, and transported there at the planter's expense.

There was no labor market. There was little money and little personal property. There was land and labor, time and tobacco. The tasks that faced these pioneers were enormous. Most of the land was heavily forested and had to be cleared by ax and ploughed by ox (or by a hand hoe). Not many ploughs were to be had, and they were crude. For a white worker, used to a colder climate, such work in the subtropical sun of Virginia's Tidewater area must have been extreme torture especially as it was required at first that all workers outside the palisades wear armor at all times.

The colony survived because, as the women came over and families became established, planters would have as many children as the high infant mortality rate would permit, and children were valuable as farm workers. They could set out the seedlings and do much of the back bending labor because they were closer to the ground than adults and also had more flexible backs. Even a little experience pulling

weeds in a Virginia tobacco field would encourage any man
to have as large a family as possible.

With this kind of labor supply, Virginia could not increase
production and meet the demand. It had quickly become evident, after the first shipment of John Rolfe's new tobacco had
met with enthusiastic approval abroad, that tobacco would
have to be the answer to Virginia's problem of survival. It
took some years, however, for it to appear that Negro labor
would have to be the answer to the problem of growing tobacco in volume.

The Spanish and Portugese had long been using African
slave labor in their West Indian and Brazilian sugar cane
industry, and in their tobacco fields as well. The Spanish
had enslaved some of the South American Indians and had
transported some North American Indians to their island
plantations where they could not escape into forests and
swamps that were familiar to them; but when world demand for tobacco exploded into such huge proportions they
quickly ran out of Indians. It was then that they sought
slaves in great numbers from Africa.[1]

Virginians did not seek Negro labor. Perhaps they would
have as time went by and competition for the world markets
grew more keen and the necessity for producing tobacco in
greater volume became more pressing, but at first, and for a
half century, the Negro was, so to speak, forced upon them.
In 1619, six years after the first ship load had sparked frantic efforts to produce the magic weed in ever greater quantities, twenty Negroes were landed at Jamestown. For a long
time people believed that it was a Dutch sea captain who
brought them and sold them as slaves to the planters, but
further research has revealed the truth, and it has been
publicized by such authorities as Matthew Page Andrews.

The captain was not a Dutchman but an Englishman. This
was not allowed to be known at the time because the Negroes had been pirated from a Spanish ship, and if news had
reached the Spanish that Jamestown was a "fence" for
stolen Spanish goods, there might have been reprisals. Nor

were these Negroes accepted as slaves for life. It is true that John Rolfe said that the captain had "sold us some negars", but the term "sold" was customarily used in speaking of the indenture of white servants for a limited period.

Lifetime slavery did not come into legal existence until more than 30 years later when, in 1653, a Negro named John Casor complained that his master, Anthony Johnson, had kept him in servitude some years longer than he should have, which was a serious offense. Johnson, frightened, released Casor from all claims against him, but then found that Casor had bound himself to one Parker who had aided him in obtaining his freedom. Johnson then sued Parker, claiming that he, Johnson, was entitled to the lifetime service of Casor, and won his case. (Johnson vs. Parker, Northampton County).[1]

This entitles Anthony Johnson to be called, "The Father of Negro Slavery in Virginia", and changes somewhat the complexion of "that peculiar institution" because Johnson himself was a Negro. And quite a fellow! Apparently one of the original 20 landed in 1619, he earned his freedom in 1623 and acquired some acreage in Accomac. He imported some servants of his own and established a community of free Negroes. Obviously, there were other free Negroes that early. However, this landmark case only shows that under the circumstances that existed, anyone white or black or otherwise would have done the same thing.[2]

Had the Indians, who "invented" tobacco, been able to look ahead a little, see what was happening, change their lifestyle accordingly and adapt themselves to the white man's ways, there would have been no slavery. The Indians could have furnished the labor and much of the management, working in cooperation with the white man, and both could have profited; but working white man's style was repugnant to the Indians, and they could not be enslaved. The deep forests were too close at hand.

The white man did not invent slavery. He didn't even invent work. Those things were here on earth before the white man came into existence as such. It can be said that the white man invented FREE labor, whereby an individual could sell his services at an agreed upon price if he could find some one who wanted to buy his services. But here, there was no free labor market, and couldn't be, because of the extremely long distances labor had to travel to get here. Ocean passage from England to Virginia cost a young man as much as seven years of hard labor under contract, and as many as four out of five, in the early years, never lived to complete their contracts. There had to be a more practical way of getting labor if Virginia was to survive.

Where, then, but along the African coast were crowds of people waiting to be picked up and transported to the places in the world where simple but vital tasks had to be performed? In Virginia the task was raising tobacco which grew in the sun, and the Negro could work in the sun without suffering heat exhaustion, sunstroke, and skin cancer. Would any pioneer people, desperate for labor to maintain themselves, their families and homes have refused to employ them when the traders brought them to the very doors of the planters?

That Negroes became slaves was inevitable because of the undeveloped state of African life. They had no influence in their own government and were sold by their own rulers to nations competing with each other for independent existence. What one nation did successfully the others had to do also or else improve upon it. The remarkable thing about slavery in Virginia is that it took so long to get established on a wide scale.

Fishwick states that in 1619, the year that the House of Burgesses first met and the first Negroes landed here, Virginia shipped out 20,000 pounds of tobacco. Three years later, in 1622, the year of the great Indian massacre, 60,000 pounds were shipped, despite the fact that one-fourth of the white population had been killed in March of that year. Five years later, in 1627, total shipments had risen to 500,000 pounds. These totals were reached obviously, without, or with very, very little, Negro labor; but when tobacco production was multiplying at such a rate to keep up with the frantic world demand, it seems surprising that more Negroes were not imported.

CHAPTER THREE

SLAVES OF TOBACCO

Since the early 1600's, there have been two kinds of slaves to tobacco: slaves to the use of it, who have represented all races and colors, and slaves to the growing of it, who have been mostly white and black.

Tobacco was first thought to have medicinal qualities, and people drank infusions of it. Powdered tobacco (snuff) was sniffed up the nostrils to clear the head, and became an elaborate social ritual. However, dipping snuff (putting a pinch of it between the lip and the gums) later became a habit on a lower social scale, as did chewing tobacco. Until about 1800 the smoking of tobacco was done almost exclusively in clay pipes, and thousands of them have been found in the diggings at colonial sites. Inhabitants of Mediterranean shores discovered that the gnarled root of their native brier made the best pipes, and it still does. Cigars became popular early but cigarettes, especially ready made ones, came later in the 19th century. Early in the 20th century, cigarette manufacturers directed much of their advertising toward making cigarette smoking attractive to women but did not dare show pictures of women actually smoking until just prior to World War II. It was that war which boosted cigarette popularity to enormous proportions, especially American brands. More recently, the federal government has exerted fanatical efforts to pressure smokers into giving up the habit, and to scare nonsmokers from taking it up. The habit has deep roots.

The secret of poise is knowing what to do with your hands, and that is the secret of kicking the tobacco habit. Your hands acquire complicated automatic patterns of activity of which you are not conscious. Your hands can sneak a cigarette out of a package, slip it between your lips and light it without your being aware of what you are doing. If you have been terrified into giving up the habit, your hands may force you to take up a worse one. And remember that smoking alters the sense of smell. When you quit smoking, things may not smell as sweet as they did, but that is the way the world is.

Those who become slaves to the growing of tobacco have a hard task master. It is a thirteen month operation. Before the old crop is completely harvested and marketed, the new crop has to be started along with seeds in flats. Later the seeds are set out in a prepared field and have to be kept free from weeds, tobacco worms and all the other agricultural pests. When harvested, the leaves have to be tied in bunches and cured in an artificially heated barn, then stored for shipment to market. Tobacco is perishable. Too dry, it crumbles into dust when handled; too moist, it rots. In the early years, there were no regularly scheduled sailings, and a crop had to be stored a long time, often, and then taken on a long voyage to England. Many a shipment arrived at its destination in worthless condition. But life in Virginia depended wholly on tobacco.

There was still no great desire for Negro labor on the part of Virginians during the 1600's until the last quarter of the century. By 1649, Virginia had only 300 Negroes in a total population of 15,000, according to Wertenbaker. They had been coming in at the rate of only 7 to 39 individuals per year during the 1630's, and not until 1653 would any of them be, legally, slaves for life. There were few plantations then that required large labor forces. About 1670, Sir William Berkeley reported to the Board of Trade that the total population of Virginia was 40,000, of whom 5% (2,000) were slaves. By 1715, the white population was estimated at 72,000, an increase of 80% over the 1670 figures; but the Negro population had increased nearly 700% to a total of 23,000. In the 60 years from 1715 to 1774 (just before the American Revolution) population figures had risen to 300,000 whites and 200,000 Negroes. The increase in Negroes reflected the peak years of importation before the trade was shut down by the war; but most of the increase was biological. Not as many slaves were brought here as is sometimes thought.[1]

The total number of Africans imported into the New World

during the 300 years the slave trade operated, has been estimated at about ten million; but only 427,000 of that number were brought to the colonies and the states during the 200 years that slavery existed here. Therefore, it is obvious that if the abolitionists had really been trying to improve the lot of the Negro race, they were working on only 4% of the problem, and on the part of it that needed the least help.[1]

By 1865, the population of American Negroes had increased ten times, but in many of the other areas in the New World, the death rate had far exceeded the birth rate and the Negro population had shrunk. One reason for this population explosion was lack of economic pressures limiting family size. Slaves had no problem of providing food, shelter, clothing and medical care for all the children that each pair of individuals could bring into the world. Better nutrition, fewer hazards and available medical attention resulted in a longer average useful life and a reduction in infant mortality. However life here compared with life in their native Africa, Negroes brought here were vastly better off than those taken to almost any other place.

By following Wertenbaker's figures, it is easy to see why importation of Negroes increased over the years. Ocean passage from England to Virginia for an indentured servant was £6 plus food and supplies on the voyage, bringing the landed cost of a white worker to about £20 which, over a five year indenture period would amount to £4 per year plus fringe benefits if the worker didn't expire before his contract did, or skip out as some did. On the other hand, a good Negro worker with a labor life expectancy of say 25 years could be had for from £18 to £30, averaging about £1 per year. This meant a reduction in the planter's labor cost of 75%, a whopping reduction, and one that enabled the Virginia planter to meet Spanish competition. Arithmetic has never been defeated. When all the costs and hazards were added up, it was found that the only way Virginia could survive in the tobacco business was to employ Negro slave labor. Negro labor put the planter's business in the black, you might say; white labor put it in the red.

But not only black slaves wore a price tag. Indentured whites had theirs too. William Matthews, with 3 years, 9 months to go on his contract, was inventoried at £12; another with 2 remaining was carried on the books at £9, while a lad with 7 years still to serve was up for £10.[1]

It may be hard now to understand why there should have been a price on the head of a worker, but the economy then and now were different things. Today the average worker has a car, perhaps a home, and some durable goods that give him a credit standing with property that can be pledged. Before the so-called Industrial Revolution, a worker had nothing he could pledge but his services. He could bind himself out for a period of time and if he didn't live up to his contract, the only recourse against him was enforced additional service or jail.

Labor is costly, has always been costly under any arrangement, but slavery tended to stabilize costs. Wages fluctuate with supply and demand, and free labor can be tempted away by rumors of richer opportunities elsewhere. A slave force is always where it is needed, and agriculture needs a labor force that is tied to the soil. This was especially true of tobacco which is not seasonal but requires year round attention. Also, under good management, slaves learned skills for lifetime use, and there was not the need for continually training new workers. These were important considerations because prices were fixed in London and taxes imposed there. The planter had no control over either.

Another reason for the declining use of indentured servants was that land in 50 acre plots was becoming scarce. Tobacco impoverishes the soil and there was no way that the nutrients it absorbed could be replaced. Neither lime nor fertilizer was available, and no means of transporting it if there had been any. The planter cleared 50 acres, planted it to tobacco for from three to seven years, then moved on to another 50 acres which had to be cleared and ready by the time needed. This created a tremendous population pressure, and planters pushed southward and westward until they burst through the mountain barrier.

Slave ownership and tobacco production, all propaganda to the contrary, were not for lovers of ease. A one-crop economy had plenty of obviously undesirable features, and tobacco had many peculiar to itself. Slavery, though adapted to tobacco production, had many internal problems that kept it from being the "you-make-the-bread-and-I'll-eat-it" sort of thing that abolitionists later claimed it to be. Not all the slaves were young, healthy, vigorous workers, and those who were didn't stay that way forever. When a planter became a slave owner, he was stuck with his slaves. He couldn't lay off his help as an employer of free labor could, or turn the old and feeble out to be supported by public charity. He couldn't find a buyer for lazy slaves or ones who couldn't work, and he wouldn't sell his good ones and keep the poor workers. If he freed a slave, he had to be responsible that the freed slave did not become a public charge. The owner, his family, the slaves and their families were all slaves of tobacco, bound to the soil of Virginia by the chains of economic necessity.

Who knows what the Virginia colony would have been without tobacco and the Negroes to grow it? Failure to follow the lead of Spain in employing Africans would have been economic suicide, and failure of the English to colonize Virginia successfully would not have benefitted the Negro. SOME people were going to settle here, if not the English, then most probably the Spanish, and the Negroes would have been slaves anyway, but under the Dons, and Spanish would have been the language of the entire continent. Depending upon your origins and sympathies you may consider this better or worse, but it seems you must admit that it would have been different.

The plantation was home to both whites and Negroes and often bred a "family" feeling among them. They were far apart, these large plantations, and amazingly self-sufficient. Members of the "family" made or grew all their basic necessities. Trade with outsiders was infrequent. People did not gad about as they do today. Distance and terrain made road building expensive, often prohibitive, and such roads as there were might be negotiable only in good weather. Southern red clay, stubbornly sticky after a rain, clinging in great gobs to one's feet, to the horse's hoofs and to the wheels of wagon or carriage, discouraged travel except when the ground was dry and hard, and the weather not too hot for the horse to get a workout. Even then, five or six miles on horseback or in a light buggy was a good hour's travel if the horse was to be spared for other work. A saddle horse walks at about 3 miles per hour, trots comfortably at six. Most saddle horses were trained to a more comfortable gait than a straight trot, but these fancy gaits were no faster.

It was isolation that made many a happy community in a plantation and created a clannish loyalty among its members, with the Negroes always included "in the family". The word "slave" was seldom used. It was "people". A Negro might identify himself, with more than a touch of pride, as "one of Col. Carey's people"; or identify the Careys as "MY people", and you'd better not say anything true or false against any of the Careys white or black. This kind of relationship had to exist to a substantial extent if the colonial venture was to become a success; and there can be no doubt that it was a success. The Southern colonies were prosperous and strong, as proved in five wars.

CHAPTER FOUR

WHAT NOBODY KNEW

Very early in their experience with Negro slavery, Virginians made attempts to end the traffic, but were always opposed by their royal governors and by the king.[1] Up to very shortly before the Revolutionary War, George III found it necessary to admonish the colonies to cease and desist in their persistent efforts to have all importations of slaves stopped. After fighting broke out, the slave trade became moribund, and the British offered freedom to American slaves in return for their aid in suppressing the colonial revolt. The British had brought them here, sold them at a profit, then as a war measure, tried to set them free, exactly as the North did four score and seven years later. (The British did carry off a number of slaves, and what happened to them might make interesting research.) But the slaves had been offered freedom before. During Bacon's Rebellion, both Bacon and Governor Berkeley offered freedom to any slaves and indentured servants who would join in the war on the proper side. As these offers were made by bands of armed men, it is presumed that the offers were accepted and that slaves served on both sides of the conflict. Tax exemptions were freely offered too, but as Bacon died in a few months and Berkeley the following year, nobody got anything that had been promised.[2]

Slavery is probably mankind's oldest and most enduring institution. It all started when some people were able to force some others to perform some disagreeable chores for them; or perhaps when some people wanted to avoid the responsibilities of freedom and sold themselves into the service of others. We shall never know. Slavery acquired some respectability when prisoners of war were put to work instead of being put to death, and the institution was accepted by the conquerors because it was more profitable than slaughter, and accepted by the enslaved because it was better than being slaughtered.

There have been many famous slaves. Aesop for one, fa-

mous for his fables 2,500 years ago; and Captain John
Smith for another. He was captured by the Turks and enslaved, but escaped. Many Greek and Roman lads received
their schooling from family slaves.

It was the Portugese, those indefatigable seafarers and
prowlers of the world's sea lanes and estuaries who, as modern times slowly emerged from medieval times, discovered
that good black workers could be bought cheap along the
African coast and sold high along other coasts. When they
and the Spanish began raising cane and making sugar in
Brazil and Cuba, and learned from the Indians how to grow
tobacco, Negroes were brought from Africa to the shores of
the New World in great numbers. Mannix states that from
1575 to 1591, 52,000 slaves were sent from Angola to Brazil
and the West Indies.[1]

The British had taken little interest in the slave trade until
they saw the increasing need in their own colonies for
African labor. The Dutch had moved in on the Portugese
and were doing fine with a virtual monopoly, so the British
moved in on the Dutch and did even better. In 1672, the
king formed the Royal African Company and put the Duke
of York at its head. It was a royal monopoly and only company ships were allowed to traffic in slaves. The business
thrived, but more and more unauthorized ships got into it,
including American ships, and there was just too much sea
surface for the Royal Navy to patrol, so the king in 1698
threw the trade open to all, with a 10% tax.[2]

There were few slaves in the British Isles, and after 1572
there weren't any. "Set foot on British soil and you're free",
or words to that effect said a judge; but slavery continued in
the British West Indies until 1833. Then it was abolished
bloodlessly with compensation to slave owners. Abolition
never became the violent political issue there that it did
here. In fact, it only became a political issue here after
1800.

The American Revolution ended in 1783, and delegates from
twelve of the thirteen colonies went into a huddle at Vir-

ginia's suggestion to develop a constitution with more effective rules than the Articles of Confederation provided. Virginia offered a number of amendments to the proposed constitution, one of which would have made further importation of slaves immediately illegal. Who should take the lead in defeating this but the New England delegates because of the profits the trade was bringing into their section. They were supported by some deep South delegates who needed more African labor for their developing cotton plantations. George Mason, who was to draft the first ten articles of the constitution as they are today, refused to sign the finished document, partly because the continuation of slavery had been guaranteed and also because another even more important amendment had not been adopted. (This to be discussed later.) The Constitution did give Congress power to end the slave trade twenty years after the Constitution's adoption.

The thinking of most delegates seemed to be that, left to the states, slavery would be phased out gradually. Few people wanted more Africans brought in and hoped that ending the trade would be the first step toward ending the institution itself. They could have been right, but there were a few things that nobody knew.

Nobody knew that the land on the other side of the Blue Ridge Mountains, granted to war veterans, would induce fully a third of Virginia's population to follow Daniel Boone through the Cumberland Gap into the County of Kentucky.

Nobody knew that all of Virginia's vast holdings, conquered by George Rogers Clark's Virginians at Virginia's sole expense would, as a result of Virginia's voluntary action, be ceded for the creation of five new states.[1]

Nobody knew that the Virginians who would people these new Western states would forget their Virginia heritage, become identified with the interests and the thinking of the new West and shift the nation's political center of gravity away from the Old Dominion.

Nobody knew how to put an end to slavery without causing financial disaster and bringing starvation to the slaves themselves who, instead of being freedom's first beneficiaries, would be its first victims.

Nobody knew that what we call the Industrial Revolution was getting ready to snowball into the 19th century and vastly alter the world's economic, political and social structure.

Nobody knew that a Yankee boy named Eli Whitney would invent a simple device in 1793 that would, over night, revolutionize the production of cotton and help make slavery an even more vital part of the economy.

Nobody knew that a Virginia boy named Cyrus McCormick would invent a device in 1831 that would eventually upset the political and economic balance some more, and make slavery obsolete without war, if people would only be patient.

But there was one thing that everybody in the South, at least, must have known or felt, an important underlying thought in the minds of serious people on the subject of emancipation however it was brought about; but nobody seems to have talked much about it. It will be discussed a little later on.

CHAPTER FIVE

AFRICA'S ONE-CROP ECONOMY

All phases of slavery have had such a thorough going over in newspapers, magazines, books, tracts, sermons, street corner harangues, novels, lectures, short stories, long stories and even TV extravaganxas that the "peculiar Institution" is popularly singled out as the most horrible of all horrors. There were, of course, other practices beside slavery that involved horrors, and slavery involved other races than African Negroes. If all the cruelties and injustices that have been dealt out by mankind could be added up and proper distribution among the races accurately calculated, who knows which race would come off with the most suffering?

At a time when white children worked fourteen hours a day in unhealthy factories and textile mills, or ran as vagabonds about the dirty streets of big cities, were hanged for petty crimes or imprisoned in filthy jails where they became hardened professional criminals, the question whether slavery was more cruel or less so than other practices becomes somewhat academic, and in any event is irrelevent to the subject in hand.

Slavery had three phases, starting, obviously, with procurement of candidates for forced labor. It is the careless habit of some commentators to talk about Southerners "enslaving Negroes", ignoring the fact that the enslaving could only have been done in Africa by Africans for a world market in which the nations of the world bid against each other. White men did not go into the interior of Africa and kidnap free Negroes. Africa was then still the "Dark Continent", and the interior was "the white man's grave". The enervating climate, the malarial swamps, thick jungles, fierce animals, poisonous snakes, hungry crocodiles, the Tsetse fly, dysentery and the fearful fevers peculiar to the tropics discouraged whites from wandering around. Few penetrated beyond the coast line, and fewer returned. Native kings and chiefs resented any kidnapping of their people by whites. It robbed them of their fees, and they would wreak murderous vengeance on offenders when this practice was tried. Native slavers also did not hesitate to capture and enslave wandering whites, and apparently there was a "white" market among the blacks.[1]

Until the Revolutionary War put a temporary end to the slave trade, most Negroes brought to America were from the interior of West Africa. They were captured by fellow Africans who were professional slave procurers. The captives were chained together in long lines and driven over jungle trails, sometimes for hundreds of miles, down to the slave coast which extended from the Cape Verde Islands at the most western tip of the African continent (the point nearest the Western hemisphere) all the way down to and including Angola below the equator, altogether about 4,000 miles or so of coast line. Here were the slave ships of many nations riding at anchor beyond the big breakers while their captains haggled with representatives of the native kings.

This enormous area of Africa was divided among native kingdoms and language groups, and further subdivided into tribal communities and villages. The native Negroes varied considerably in coloring and facial as well as other features. The native kings wielded despotic power by having many sons by many wives and surrounding themselves with officials who were members of the royal family. All had slaves of their own.[2]

A one-crop economy supported all the native kingdoms on the West African coast, and that one crop was slaves. There were by-products like ivory, gold, palm oil, brought down to the coast by the slaves and sold along with those who brought them, but export of slaves was the main enterprize. For more years than we know, this section of Africa had furnished slaves in untold numbers to the rest of the world; and to the New World there had been traffic for 150 years before the first Negroes were brought to Virginia.

The shrewd native leaders, skilled in all the tricks of the trade, knew how to haggle and get top prices for their human wares. They had slaves of their own and often sold some of them off to the white strangers in the big ships. Thus, many of the Negro newcomers to America had been slaves from birth. African kings, justifying their exportations of fellow Africans, claimed that they were only disposing of prisoners of war; but few purchasers had any illusions that the so-called wars were anything but raids for the procurement of prisoners.

After the sick and the weak in the long lines trudging down the trail to the sea had been cut loose and left for the jungle predators, those who made it to the water's edge were terrified by the pounding sea, the tall groaning ships with big sails like wings of gigantic birds of prey. Wild rumors circulated among them concerning their ultimate fate.

These candidates for overseas job opportunities would be held in closely guarded enclosures until a bargain could be reached between their captors and the ship's captain. Then they would be packed into big canoes and paddled by skilled native crews out through the great breakers and hoisted aboard a waiting ship. Most of the poor creatures had never seen a white man before a prospective purchaser looked them over in the enclosure and made his choices from among them. They could have had no idea what lay beyond nor why they had been torn from their homes and delivered into the awful ships. It was natural for them to suppose that they were to be eaten by giants.

On the other hand, the native kings and chiefs and their tribesmen who did the rounding up were in constant contact with American, British, and European men who had advantages that Africans lacked, and they knew something of other cultures. They were trading their own people for guns, knives, gaudy textiles, tools, trinkets and liquor, and they could have had anything they wanted in return for what they were selling to the iron men in wooden ships.

Negro kings and chieftains got rich, but in all the centuries of trading with western nations they showed no interest in building manufacturing plants for producing the things for which they were enslaving and bartering their own people.

They knew about the white man's books but developed no literature or written language of their own. They knew about western cities and saw the forts along their own coasts but took no interest in architecture or science. Nothing sparked a desire to improve their own lot or the lot of the wretched victims of their greed. Trading in slaves brought riches to Britain which were used for the improvement of living conditions there. The same trade brought riches to African kings but were used to import luxuries for the kings themselves. No native patriot came forward to liberate his people from their tyrants, and no Negro Stephen Langton emerged to write a set of rules for African freedom.

The harsh environment of jungles and swamps, oppressive climate and fevers protected inhabitants of Africa's interior from white raiders, and Africa's people had developed ability to survive those hazards. Surrounding Africa was a world of restless energy, stirred to a spirit of pioneering by the discovery of a new world with fabulous possibilities but a population vacuum. Africa, teeming with people, was a power vacuum. Nature abhors a vacuum. The powers of Europe were drawn to Africa, and Africa's people were drawn up into the current of "progress", against their will, to be sure, but if they had developed as the people in most of the other countries had, they could have freed themselves from their despotic rulers and maintained their integrity against the outside world behind their protective environment.

Why didn't they? Why weren't they competitive with other nations when they had their climate working for them? If they couldn't be free then, what are the chances now for the success of newly created African nations thrust into existence by self interested politicians and involved in complex international intrigue for which they have had no preparation and have exhibited little natural aptitude?

No longer is Africa "the white man's grave". Modern science has made it possible for other races to survive there, and Africa is again a vacuum, made so by the pull-out of its former colonial powers. Aggressive communism has expanded by skillful infiltration into every vacuum that has opened up since World War II. Will Africa be thrust back into slavery, not slavery Western style, but slavery Siberian style?

CHAPTER VI:

MIDDLE PASSAGE

Phase two of the slavery phenomenon was the transportation of slaves from the African coast to their destination in the New World. It was the second leg of a great triangle, a three-cornered sea journey that began and ended at the slave ship's home port. A British ship would set out for Africa from, say, Liverpool with a cargo including whiskey, textiles, firearms, cutlasses and such other items that experienced slavers knew would intrigue the slave-gathering native chiefs. After taking on its live cargo in Africa, the ship would sail for a West Indies port, unload, clean up and take on rice, sugar, tobacco and later cotton, then sail for home and another go-round. An American ship would sail from, say, Salem Massachusetts (said to have been the home port of more slavers than any other). The bargaining cargo would include rum instead of whiskey because rum was cheaper and just as good for trading. The American ship might be anchored right alongside a British ship and take slaves from the same enclosure, sail for the same port and take on the same cargo for its homeward journey, except that it would have hogsheads of molasses for conversion into rum by the New England distilleries for more slave trading. The second leg of the triangle, carrying the slaves from Africa to their destination, was known as the "Middle Passage".

Two careful students of the period have dipped their pens in acid to preserve a graphic picture of certain transportation details. They note that, generally, the type of vessel in use in New England's slave commerce was one of some fifty tons burden. It was sixty to seventy feet in length. The space between decks, occupied by the human cargo on the one to two months voyage to the shores of the new world, was from three feet, six inches, to three feet, ten inches. Throughout the interminable voyage, except for limited periods in daylight when trusties were brought above deck for air and exercise, the shackled slaves had to sit or to lie down. It is not to be wondered that, during the indescribable "Middle Passage", passenger mortality averaged eight to ten per cent. Considering the close confinement, the cramped quarters, the duration of the passage, the heat between decks, the seasickness, the inevitable insanitary surroundings, the imagination is beggared by the effort to grasp the torture involved.

Blood money it was, but it was also easy money. The glint of gold had wrought a startling transformation; humanitarian impulses had faded out under its withering blight. The lure of profit converted the erstwhile oppressed into ruthless oppressors. They who had braved the perils of the sea in flight from persecution were now plying the same waters in a commerce that robbed other men of liberty. The land of the free was to become the home of the slave.

A New England historian records that the Puritans of Massachusetts carried on a large trade in negroes with the Guinea chiefs. He quotes the Boston News Letter as stating that during the decade of 1755 to 1766, the importers landed on the shores of Massachusetts no fewer than twenty-three thousand blacks. According to the same writer, Massachusetts alone, in the single year 1750, used in this traffic fifteen thousand hogsheads of rum. Furthermore, the theretofore unheard-of profits dulled the consciences of the faithful to such an extent that such moral scruples as existed relative to the retention of the slaves on sacred Massachusetts soil died out into complaisant acquiescence with their sale to colonists in the South.

Nor was Massachusetts alone in activity in the trade in negroes. In 1750, Newports' fleet of slavers numbered one hundred and seventy vessels. Connecticut had a part in the new commerce. A New Englander commented in 1787 that Rhode Island then held first place in the traffic in African negroes, that the trade constituted one of the colony's leading activities and was the source of the wealth of the majority of its citizens. Governor Hopkins is authority for the record that for three decades prior to 1764 the colony sent annually to Africa some eighteen ships laden with eighteen hundred hogsheads of rum. Although its lawmakers took pains in 1774 to decorate its statute books with an act reciting that any slave thereafter brought into the colony should immediately become free, they were foresighted enough to tack on as an appendage a convenient escape clause; namely, that in certain specified instances emancipation would not be enforced provided the importer would give bond conditioned to dispose of the slaves beyond the boundaries of the colony. By which happy arrangement the Rhode Islanders salved their consciences and saved their investments.

It can be seen that the slave trade required financing in large amounts. Wealthy men bought shares in slaving expeditions. A ship had to be bought, fitted out, loaded with trade goods, provisioned and manned with captain and crew. Half the wages of officers and men were advanced at sailing time, the rest held back and paid out of monies received from the sale of slaves when the ship reached home port. Those who advanced the money wanted it back with a handsome profit. There were many risks involved, but investment opportunities then were few and none without some element of risk. There was no stock market, and Wall Street was a muddy little lane running from a grave yard to a river, but money could not be allowed to lie idle. Even Peter Faneuil, who donated Faneuil Hall, the "Cradle of Liberty" in Boston, was a major financier in at least one slaving venture.[2]

After 1808, the slave trade was illegal, but that didn't stop it. It sent the price of slaves up and made the lot of live cargoes on the middle passage even worse, as greedy men, desperate for big money, took daring chances. British and American vessels patrolled the seas but could only occasionally capture a ship loaded with Negroes, and that often only made things worse for the unfortunates. The Negroes had to be put ashore in Africa, perhaps Liberia, and it was like throwing drowning men back into the water. Liberians didn't want them except as slaves and often drove the homeless souls off where their fate must have been far worse than where they would have been taken in the first place.

The illegal slavers who got through with their cargoes (and that included most of them) could only land on the Spanish islands. All British and American ports were closed to slave ships. They would unload their cargoes secretly at night; and in the dark, from secret coves and swamps small fast boats would slip out and smuggle a few individuals at a time to secret accomodations on other islands or the mainland where they could be maintained secretly until they could be made ready for sale as legitimate slaves. This procedure portended a smuggling operation on a grand scale a century or more later when foreign ships lined up outside the three mile limit of our shores during prohibition times, and small, fast "rum runners" would slip out at night and ferry bottles instead of blacks to secret places on the shore.

As patrols became more effective with more and faster ships, slavers took their business to the African east coast. Slaves were cheaper in the markets of Madagascar and Zanzibar, enough so to justify the long trip around the Cape of Good Hope, but the return trip, the middle passage, imposed additional suffering upon the live cargo. The longer the ships were at sea, the more storms were encountered when hatches had to be battened down in suffocating heat, and the more chance there was of dread diseases breaking out among cargo and crew. The law that was supposed to improve conditions was having the opposite effect. Many laws are still being made for political purposes and then not enforced for practical purposes.

CHAPTER VII:

DISPLACED PERSONS

Phase three of the slavery triangle was the final disposition of the slaves at their destination. For those who arrived here in America, after phases one and two, the auction block could not have held many terrors. Released from the hold of a cramped, ill-smelling ship, washed up, well fed and made presentable for sale, they must have experienced a feeling of relief. Certainly the auction block could not have produced in them the same sensations that a sightseer today would experience if suddenly put up for sale under 17th, 18th or early 19th century conditions.

The newcomers to these shores saw their own kind standing about, some dressed much as were the white people and seemingly as free, all without spears or hostile attitudes. Rumors current in Africa that the captives were to be eaten by giant cannibals must have lost their credence. After the sale, which they couldn't have understood, they found themselves on an American plantation among others from the "old country", perhaps even kinsmen, and probably encountered the first kind word and friendly attention that had come their way since the fearful night when they were dragged from their huts in their humble village.

It was at this point that slavery Southern style began and the slave trade Yankee style, Dutch, British, Spanish, Portugese, French, Danish, Arabian or African left off; but strangely enough it is from here that the Uncle Tom's Cabin fans revel in recounting fictional versions of Negroes oppressed, beaten, brutalized and "de-humanized" (whatever de-humanization is, unless it is transforming Negroes by some necromancy or black magic into hideous beings without souls, but if so, what kind of soul transplant technique did abolitionist science have that would "re-humanize" them?)

Two questions arise here: (1) What was so "de-humanizing" about association with the Southern planter and his family;

and (2) If the Negroes were adversely affected by slavery Southern style, they must have enjoyed a more edifying existence previously and if so, when did they?

Without a definition of "de-humanization" or an explanation of how it manifested itself, it would be reasonable to assume that slavery on almost any Southern plantation would have to be an improvement on the Negroes' immediate past experience, their forced march down the jungle trails, incarceration on the beach awaiting an unknown fate, and their life on shipboard. Association with their captors, the men who took them from their homes and handled them like animals, and those who held them behind the beach barricades, plus the crew on the ship, could not have been very elevating. Home, however wretched, must have seemed in retrospect like paradise in comparison, but if the tortures they experienced en-route hadn't robbed them of their humanity, they surely didn't lose it on a Southern plantation, and they always seemed to be human enough there. The only time when any of them became otherwise was when aroused to crime by some fanatic, and that happened very seldom.

They may still have yearned for home and old associations in Africa, but how much and for how long no one knows. They adapted, and after that would they have preferred their previous life to their new existence? Some revealing comments were made by Charles Francis Adams who was hardly to be charged with prejudice against the Negro. He was of the Massachusetts Adamses (and up there you take your hat off before you utter the name of Adams). The Adams family was a distinguished family and Charles was a distinguished Adams, a Union Army brigadier, a brave and chivalrous soldier, a scholar, an observant traveler, an honest man and a grandson of President John Quincy Adams. He visited Africa and saw at first hand how Africans lived. He was impressed with the "appalling amount of error" and "self sufficient ignorance" in which Americans and especially his own New Englanders had indulged. He found that where Negroes had been "left to their own devices", living conditions had remained the same generation after generation without change or improvement over conditions described by travelers many decades previously.[1]

In the 1960's, a television series called "Wild Cargo" showed pictures and gave descriptions of African village life in modern times. The show was not propaganda, nor political in any way. It was put on by a professional hunter and collector of specimens for scientific purpoes. The glimpses of African native life were incidental but it was impossible not to notice the primitive conditions that prevailed. The only visible improvement was in the clothes that some of the natives were wearing.[2]

Perhaps there was nothing to inspire ambition for self improvement, and the Africans wanted none. Maybe their way of life suited them fine. There had been no one to tell them that change was desirable and that they ought to be dissatisfied with life as it was, or that they deserved better treatment from those above and around them. Perhaps it would have been cruel to make these people dissatisfied.

It is too bad that the feelings of the "displaced persons" brought to America, could not have been learned at first hand, but no reporters from the Washington Post or the Boston Globe were at the dock when the barefoot blacks shuffled down the gangplank. Nobody interviewed them and asked their views on African politics, how they liked America, how conditions here compared with those of their native land, and if they would like to go back. If their impressions could have been gathered while their experiences were fresh, their answers would have been uninfluenced by propaganda, and much might have been learned. Later on, when they were interviewed, many of the interviewers were not so much interested in the truth as in supporting their own theories; and after the Negroes had taken on a degree of sophistication, and had found out what their questioners wanted to hear, they gave answers that were not supposed to reveal the truth so much as to please themselves and their interviewers.

One thing seems certain. If the American Negro, after being here long enough to see what this country was like, did yearn for freedom, it was not the kind of freedom he knew in Africa but the kind he saw around him here, or perhaps the idealized kind of freedom painted by abolition zealots. Certain it is too, that the young Negroes born outside of Africa, knew nothing at first hand about village life in "the old country", and their elders seem to have neglected to tell them much about it. They weren't taught to cherish African institutions and conditions, as people of other national backgrounds usually were. Some part of their old life did cling and survive passing generations. The "ha'nts" and the omens, the "sperrits" that they told the young white children about, and the personalities of birds, animals and even inanimate objects had a distinctive flavor derived from their origin abroad, and became an invaluable part of Southern American folklore.

CHAPTER VIII:

ABOLITIONISM

An obvious question is: WHY did abolitionists concentrate their efforts on phase three of the slavery cycle when phases one and two were so much worse? The answer to this would take us a little out of sequence. Some important things happened during the fifty years between the end of the Revolution and the beginning of the radical abolition movement in America. The war had changed things.

Virginia veterans of the war were eligible for grants of land beyond the Appalachian range of mountains in the territory that Virginia's George Rogers Clark had won, and by 1790, there were 74,000 people in Kentucky including 13,000 Negroes. By the year 1800, Vermont, Kentucky and Tennessee had been admitted to the Union, and the total population of all 16 states was nearly 5 & 1/2 million souls. The Louisiana Purchase had not been made, Florida had not been purchased from Spain, and the whole Southwest still belonged to Mexico; but the era of enormous expansion was about to begin, and sectional rivalry was growing. The hostility of the commercial North toward the agricultural South was manifest in opposition to the Lousiana Purchase in 1803 and in threats of secession over Madison's war policy in 1813 (Hartford Convention 1814). Slavery was not then an issue. Few wanted more Negroes imported.

But inventive genius was stirring in America, Britain and Europe, and what is called the Industrial Revolution was on its way with results that could not be anticipated. Greatly improved machines for spinning and weaving were producing more textiles for more people at less cost, and creating a demand for more cotton. Eli Whitney's cotton gin was making it possible for the Southern plantations to process more cotton for the market, and this created a need for more slaves to plant it, cultivate it and pick it. Here was the same kind of sudden, insatiable demand that tobacco had created a century and a half before, and another one-crop economy had fixed itself upon the South, this time mostly on the deep South.

Coincidental with the demand for more slaves, Congress exercised the power specifically granted it by the Constitution and passed laws ending the importation of slaves by the year 1808. Britain had made it illegal for British ships to engage in the trade after 1807; but both nations were slow in adopting enforcement measures.

So what always happens when there is an increasing demand for something and the government makes its importation illegal? Although smuggling is as old as official restrictions on imports, and that is probably as old as the stones in the Pyramids, nobody seemed to foresee that slaves would be smuggled into the country. Slave imports had been resumed legally after the Revolution and were as big a business as ever, and it kept right on after it was illegal. After the War of 1812, slave importation increased in response to the demands of cotton production. The Industrial Revolution was aggravating the evil that it would make obsolete later, but nobody foresaw that either.

There was, however, no longer any need for slaves in the North, and the states made laws for the gradual emancipation of all slaves by 1840. Negroes in the North performed no vital services that white people couldn't perform just as well. Northern economy would not have been seriously affected if Negroes there had suddenly packed up and left. Nevertheless, it was and still is asserted that if the Northerners could abolish slavery, why couldn't the Southerners? But was Northern emancipation a great and generous gesture? In history, it always pays to look for selfish motives.

Owners had a responsibility for their slaves that they couldn't shirk. They had to feed and care for them through sickness and in health until death or a bill of sale relieved them of the responsibility. If an owner freed a slave, he had to see that the individual did not become a charge upon the state, and before he made a sale he had to find a buyer. He couldn't sell old and feeble or sick slaves and keep only young and healthy ones, that is, under ordinary conditions.

The law in Northern states now made it possible for owners to get rid of all. They could now sell their good workers to Southern owners, and dump the others legally, thus ridding themselves of a liability.

The census of 1840 showed that there were 170,000 Negroes in all the Northern states, all free by then. That same year there were 198,000 free Negroes in the Southern states (Chart No.7). These were not freed by law but by the generosity of their owners, plus their proven ability to make their own way as free individuals. There was no other way at the time. Many were freed by will but then the heirs had to be responsible. General Lee, when a colonel in the U.S.Army, had to take a furlough to settle the estate of his father-in-law whose will freed all his slaves.[1]

When it is considered that freeing a slave involved considerable expense, it should also be remembered that there were 9,565,000 white people in the Northern states in 1840, and only 4,609,000 whites in the Southern states (ignoring the District of Columbia). With fewer than half the number of people to bear the expense, the South had freed in the same space of time, 16% more slaves than had the North (Chart No.7). By 1860, there were 257,000 free Negroes in the South, an increase of 30% in twenty years.[2]

In 1803, the vast land area owned by the French was purchased from Napoleon. The North, anticipating that this new area would be Southern in politics, opposed the purchase. Nothing was said about slavery. Acquisition, however, was followed by more and more people from the North and South moving westward, although most of them were from the South. At the same time, we were having difficulties with both the French and the British who were at war with each other. We settled our differences with the French peacefully by the Lousiana Purchase, and tried to settle with the English by going to war.

The war was supposed to establish "freedom of the seas", but that principle put both American and British patrol vessels in a sticky spot when they tried to apprehend slave smugglers. A captain could be in plenty of trouble if he overhauled and searched the wrong ship. The smugglers knew it and always carried a bag of flags and hoisted the appropriate one when a suspected patrol vessel hove into sight. It has never been quite clear just what was won in that war other than a clear title to the Louisiana Purchase which was not supposed to have been one of the objectives.

Andrews (pp.398/9) calls attention to a universally overlooked provision in the Treaty of Ghent that hostilities would not end until ratification by both Washington and London, a clever ruse on the part of Britain. London had never acknowledged the legality of Spain's transfer of the area to France, and therfore regarded the U.S. title as invalid. If Britain had won the Battle of New Orleans and established their own government over the whole area as they planned to do, the treaty of peace would not have been ratified by Washington and the war would have continued.

Or would it? With Britain strongly entrenched and their navy in the Gulf controlling the Mississippi River, reconquest of the area would have been extremely difficult. Northern federalists had not supported the war, and it was suggested in Massachusetts that a separate peace be signed, which would have meant secession of the Bay State. Would they have reversed themselves and joined the South in a desperate effort to drive the British out? If not, could the South have done it alone? If so, what then would the Union have been like? If not, and the British had maintained their control there, the opportunity for specualtion is far too vast for exploitation here.

It was not until somewhere around 1840 that the aggressive abolition effort began to gather momentum, its spokesmen insisting that all slaves in the South be set free. As mentioned before, abolition of slave importation had been attempted by Virginia repeatedly during the 1600's and 1700's. The Quakers had opposed slavery as early as 1700, although William Penn had owned slaves. It was a Quaker, Benjamin Lundy, who made a moral issue out of abolition and enlisted William Lloyd Garrison. Lundy urged gradual emancipation and colonization outside the country, but the rabid Garrison demanded instant, unconditional freedom for all slaves. He split with Lundy, secured financial backing, published "The Liberator" in 1831, and gathered a following. He also sparked a violent hostility among his own people in the North, but he persisted. His program offered advantages to the industrialists whose power was growing.

His propaganda became more widespread and the oratory grew more fiery. The clergy soon saw possibilities in joining the exciting game of calling down fire from heaven upon the collective head of Southern slaveholders. Phillips Brooks and Henry Ward Beecher were notable examples of preachers whose reputations as orators depended upon their zeal in denouncing the South and Southerners for "enslaving" the Negro. Child labor abuses in Northern textile mills would have been a more appropriate topic, susceptible of personal investigation and direct action, but it might have robbed the collection plate of a substantial portion of its yield because too many mill owners sat in the congregation and listened with rapt attention to anti-slavery declamations. They didn't want to hear anything about their own mill hands.[1]

Not all the clergy involved themselves in the anti-slavery movement. There were some who spoke out against the hysteria and tried to make some level-headed views apparent to the public, but they never seemed to attract enough financial backing to accomplish very much. Vermont Bishop the Right Reverend John Henry Hopkins took his fellow clergy to task, reminding them that it was not too difficult "to gratify an audience when the supposed sins of which they were under no temptation to commit, were made the subject of censure", and that "when the public mind is sufficiently heated, the politician lays hold of the subject and makes the anti-slavery movement the watchword of party". (Whether the moral or political issue came first is a point of further discussion.)[1]

Southern clergy also took part in the propaganda war. The Rev. Josiah Priest published "The Bible Defense of Slavery" in 1852 which, though it does little for the subject it purports to expound, shows that realities of the problem were being understood in the South. He said that abolitionists had done much to raise a tumult among the people with a view to winning their way to political power, and that when that was accomplished there would be two disinct governments. He shuddered at "all the horrors of such an event" because Southerners were determined to hold the rights guaranteed them by the constitution. He mentioned "the pretended sympathy" of abolitionists for the Negro, and that people were taking for granted as truth all the stories of atrocities perpetrated upon the bodies and souls of slaves. The Rev. Priest was "a Northern gentleman".

But there was little the Northern opponents of the massive anti-slavery propaganda could do. In 1859, a Southern U.S. senator toured the principal cities in New England at his own expense, pleading for an understanding of the South's problems, and came back with a feeling of accomplishment and an honorary degree from Bowdoin College, Maine; but the rapidly rising tide of anti-Southern feeling under professional direction and lavish financing engulfed the North and swept away the good the senator had accomplished. His name was Jefferson Davis.

Survival of the Republican Party depended upon war, and eagerness for victory at the polls destroyed all reason. Agitation of the kind indulged in by the abolitionists inevitably leads to acts of violence by people who let their zeal take over and lead them to extremes. Such people see visions and hear the Lord tell them in a dream to commit murder.

In 1831, Nat Turner organized some other slaves into a band that murdered 61 white people, mostly women and children in Southampton County, Virginia. Another slave, Gabriel Prosser, planned a similar massacre but a loyal slave exposed the plot and saved some innocent lives. Prosser escaped but was recognized by two other slaves on a river boat. They informed the captain, but he, an anti-slavery man, refused to turn him in. They then, at great personal risk, turned him in themselves. John Brown and his sons had the insane idea of arming some slaves with steel tipped pikes, and seized the U.S. armory at Harper's Ferry, where they killed an innocent free Negro. Brown was financed by some prominent Northerners including Thomas Wentworth Higginson and Samuel Howe, husband of Julia Ward Howe. Here was unquestionable treason, for which Brown was hanged. His financiers were not. Less violent but just as far from the centers of reason, was the slave Harriet Tubman, who is credited with managing the escape of 300 slaves through the "underground railroad". There were other similar efforts.[1]

Atrocities and deliberately hostile actions never help solve a problem, and those of the abolitionists were only hit-and-run harassment tactics, and their only effect was to stir up resentment and make co-operative measures impossible. Any people anywhere resent invasion of interlopers with the purpose of stirring up animosities.

Perhaps the most amazing thing about public reaction to these futile tactics is the fact that nobody, then or since, seems to have asked why these zealots didn't start slave revolts in Africa, the mother country of slavery. Nobody ever wondered why African natives didn't rise up against their kings and chieftains who were enslaving and exporting them. If those in the New World were heroes, why weren't there any heroes in Africa where conditions were worse and where heroes were most needed? Why didn't some abolitionist look about him and say, "We are fighting the wrong war in the wrong place. Slavery started in Africa and it will have to end there. No matter what we do here it will go on forever. Besides, we are dealing with less than 5% of total New World slavery. So Let's recruit some ex-slaves and launch a drive in Africa to destroy the power of the rulers there and eliminate the source of slaves for all areas of the world."

If this sounds fantastic and impractical, remember that these were the times of William Walker, leader of the filibusters who conquered Nicaragua and defeated the armies of five other nations. They were also the times of the attempted colonization of American Negroes sponsored by James Monroe, John Marshall, Bushrod Washington and, later, Abraham Lincoln. Liberia was founded by treaties with native princes and was to be a paradise for ex-slaves and a shining example of Negro accomplishment. Couldn't Liberia have been a good jumping-off place for abolitionists in a war against African enslavers that might have been the death of slavery? These were the times too, of British abolition agitation under William Wilberforce which succeeded in 1833 in freeing all slaves in British colonies, but compensating owners for them. Britain might even have offered active cooperation.

It is less amazing but just as significant that abolitionists did not take any effective measures to stop the building of slave ships in New England ship yards, or put an end to the distilling of rum and the manufacture of merchandise obviously designed for bartering with African slavers. According to Mannix (p.160) as early as the 1750's there were 63 distilleries in Massachusetts and 30 in Rhode Island busy converting molasses into rum for the trade. When an import duty was levied on molasses, the duty was never collected because it was claimed that it would ruin the slave trade, throw 5,000 men out of work and cause 700 ships to rot.[1]

These are amazing figures but they high-light an amazingly little known fact: THE BIG PROFIT IN THE SLAVE TRADE WAS NOT IN BRINGING SLAVES TO OUR SOUTHERN PLANTATIONS. For every ONE slave brought here, more than TWENTY were carried to Brazil, Cuba and the West Indies. So why is it that all the invective inspired by mention of the word "slaver" is always heaped upon the heads of Southerners who represented so minute a portion of the problem and had the least to do with the evils of the institution?[2]

With the Northern industrial group making money financing the slave trade and also by processing the products of slave labor, is it any wonder that they didn't want slavery or the slave trade ended? But if they didn't want slavery ended, why were they financing the abolitionists?

The answer is that the industrialists knew that the abolitionists were not going to end slavery. The industrialists were realists; the abolitionists were not. But the abolition movement was creating a climate for war, and that was what the industrialists wanted. It was as simple as that, too simple for most people to appreciate.

Financial support for fanatics usually comes from those who find that they can use the fanatics for some practical purpose, though the fanatics may not be aware of the objectives their backers have in mind. Crusaders are blinded by the dazzle of the goal they imagine and are glad to get help from any source. Of course the abolitionists received money from churches and charities and the misguided public.

There is a wide-spread movement today among political and church groups to have all economic aid denied South Africa, and all U.S. investments there ended. An article by John Train in the November 1978 Forbes Magazine reports on an interview with Gatsha Buthelezi, prominent South African black leader. Among other things, he is quoted as saying that the "uninformed liberal abroad" had things "upside down"; that foreign investments were just what his people most needed. They meant jobs. He said that American liberals who would like to see a violent confrontation in his country were working for the very thing that everybody there most wanted to avoid. For black and white, the need is for peaceful change, he is convinced, and suspects that these outside liberals are advocating policies that are not for reasons having much to do with the struggle of his people but are projections of political and emotional needs of their own. He thinks their opinions "seem to flow from THEIR politics, THEIR needs, THEIR conditions", and he expressed the wish that these people would vent their talents on some other battlefield. It is too bad that a black leader with some of Buthelizi's ideas did not arise in America in the 1850's.

Any course the American abolitionists could have adopted other than the one they did, would have made better sense, been more honest, and might have accomplished good. Killing off African kings, for instance, would have done more for Africa AND America than killing fellow Americans, and it could have been the means of uniting the country instead of splitting it apart.

But the abolitionists had to base their activities on the notion that all Southern slaves were yearning for freedom and that they, the abolitionists, were helping the helpless to achieve their most ardent desires. They overlooked the fact that freedom had been no great boon to Northern Negroes who were mostly living in miserable conditions; and it is not prominently on record that the abolitionists did much to help Northern Negroes. The public didn't ask if Southern slaves were yearning for freedom or why they should be. What was out there in the free world to attract them? What job opportunities existed in the agricultural South for anybody without capital? Even with capital, the life of the small farmer, white or black, was something not everybody would look forward to.

The standing offer on some plantations that any slave who could prove his ability to make a living in the free world could have his freedom was seldom taken advantage of. There was little incentive for a slave to improve his ability when opportunities were so scarce. A great deal needed to be done in a climate of friendly cooperation if the transition from slave to free labor was to be successful, but the abolitionists had made this impossible. They were defeating their avowed purpose (but not their real one.)

Many still believe that all runaway slaves were fleeing from oppression and that those who aided them were heroes in the cause of freedom; but how much do we really know about the "Underground railroad"? Apparently, no reliable records were kept and we do not know how many slaves were brought North nor how they fared afterward. Were they established in profitable pursuits? Did they find themselves better off? Were things in the North to their liking? Did any go back? Some very old "I-want-to-go-back" songs still survive. What inspired them? One song that old people with ante-bellum memories used to sing went in part:

> I've hoed in fields of cotton
> I've worked upon the river
> And I always thought if I got away
> I would go back, no never!
> But times have changed the old man
> My head is bending low
> My heart turns back to Dixie
> And I must go.

And Virginia had laws to permit a free Negro to become a slave and choose his own master. Some free Negroes must have become disillusioned.

But legends and sentiment aside, we know that there would have been the inevitable malingerers, trouble makers and good-for-nothing non-workers among the escapees. However, as there is no way of determining how many, suppose that all were good workers. They would have to be replaced on the plantations, and that would mean additional business for the slave traders and a zero result for the "liberators". But that is not all. It is not even the worst. The whole operation appears pretty sleazy when it is remembered that the operation was financed by Northern industrialists who also financed the illegal slave trade.

Claims are made that the "underground railroad" brought 25,000 to 100,000 slaves out of the South, but such figures are impossible. The Northern Negro population increased by 60,000 (up from 180,000 to 240,000) during the twenty years between 1840 and 1860, a one-third increase. This seems scarcely more than Mother Nature and father time could accomplish all by themselves.

During the same twenty years, the population of free Negroes in the South also increased by 60,000 (up from 198,000 to 257,000). Obviously, then, the number of slaves (whatever it was) who were freed by Northern "liberators" was matched by the number freed in the South by slave owners voluntarily manumitted their slaves, but with the difference that those freed in the South did not have to be replaced by new imports.

The people operating these escape schemes had no expectation of solving the problem of slavery. No logical course of action would have satisfied them. They deliberately demanded the impossible so that they could continue being heroes in their own imagination. They believed that they were helping to bring on a war and they gloried in it. Actually, however, they could not have brought on the war by themselves because the Northern people would not have gone to war just to free the slaves, but many (though not all) religious leaders, politicians and large numbers of the public lauded their efforts. The industrialists subsidized them.

Perhaps it is too bad that the efforts of the "underground railroad" were not more successful. If a substantial number of slaves had been brought North for the Northern people to find homes and employment for and see that they didn't become disillusioned and hard to control, if they had, say, quadrupled the Northern Negro population, they still would not have made a dent in the nearly four million slaves in the South but they might have brought about a more realistic attitude on the part of the Northern public. A new approach to the slavery problem could have swept fanaticism off the scene and made room for cool heads to operate. Violence might have been postponed long enough for the forces of economics to accomplish solutions. Industrialization in the South would have solved the tariff problem, and development of farm machinery would have eroded slavery. The "war party", however, did not want peaceful solutions.

The slave population in the South increased 60% from 1840 to 1860, but the large area acquired from Mexico accounted for much of that. The Southern white population increased by 78% from 4.6 million to 8.2 million. The cotton growing states attracted large numbers from other areas of the nation. European immigration swelled the Northern white population which increased by 100%, but few came to the agricultural South. A half million men in the Northern armed forces were foreign born.

Efforts in the South to get new states admitted as slave states was entirely political and not at all for the purpose of spreading slavery among people who didn't want it. Southerners mistakenly believed that new slave states would stand with the old ones against the ambitions of the industrial states to dominate the country.

On the other hand, contrary efforts to have new states admitted as "free soil" were not motivated by moral opposition to slavery, but were also political as well as social and economic. People in the West did not want an incursion of Negroes, and there was the fear fostered by radical speeches, including Lincoln's, that free labor could not compete with slave labor in the new areas opening up. People did not then realize that slave labor could only be successful in raising cotton and tobacco.

CHAPTER IX:

BEHIND THE FAN

A favorite topic for behind-the-fan conversation has always been interracial peccadilloes, and despite Victorian taboos, the subject was given blatant publicity during the Age of Vituperation. The slave owner was depicted as a lecherous tyrant with a seraglio of captive females; and the entire white male population of the South was accused by the more ambitious denunciators of regularly taking their pleasure at the expense of African female chastity. This titilliating subject still commands an attentive and credulous audience.

If any substantial amount of this interesting gossip had been true, there would have been, in that pre-pill era, a rather large admixture of Southern white blood in the Negro population, exemplified by a high percentage of mulatto offspring, and a rather larger percentage of mulattoes among slaves than among free Negroes.

So, as a popular politician of the past used to say, "Let's look at the record". The record is the 1860 census, which took count of mulattoes as distinct from "blacks". It provides separate totals and breakdowns, and makes the picture look very different after the smears have been rubbed off.[1]

The percentage of mulattoes was lowest in the deep South (see Chart 4) at 8% except in Louisiana where it was 13%. The percentage increased northward to 17% in Virginia (including West Virginia) and reached 20% in Kentucky. The overall average of mulattoes to blacks was 12%. The percentage of free Negroes to the total Negro population breaks down to show that 2% of the blacks were free, but 19% of the mulattoes were free.

A wide variety of physical, and other characteristics among Negroes brought here from Africa was noted at the time of importation, and it was estimated then that at most only 80% of the native Africans were "true" Negroes, meaning, evidently, that 80% conformed in general to the color and cast of facial features generally accepted as "typical". Some estimates of "true" Negroes upon arrival ran as low as 60%.

Everywhere in the South except Kentucky and Missouri, according to the 1860 census, the percentage of "true" Negroes exceeded 80%, and in these two states it was right on the nose. Therefore, if only 80% of the newly arrived Negroes were truly Negroid types, then these Africans became more typically negroid after they had been in the South a few generations than they had been in their original home land. This adds an unexpected twist to the enigma, but it is quite logical. If Negroes were of mixed blood when they arrived here, and then intermarried only among themselves with little or no alien blood being added, many of their non-negroid characteristics would disappear in a surprisingly few generations. You can't defeat biology.[1]

Of course, the percentages given were somewhat speculative. No one knows exactly how accurate the early estimates were, nor exactly where the dividing line between "blacks" and mulattoes was, in the minds of the census takers; but these figures came from people with wide familiarity with Negroes, and who had no incentive for falsifying. What the newly imported Negroes were like was reported by people interested, it can be assumed, only in the economic value of workers. Certainly the census takers were merely trying to record the facts, get their job done, and didn't waste time trying to prove theories. Their estimates, as are all such, were subject to human error, but the error would be the same in both cases, so that the basis for comparison between the time of importation and the time of the census several generations later, would remain essentially the same.

American Negroes came from a number of different sections of Africa, areas spread over many thousands of square miles and varying in climate, terrain and natural resources. The people varied just as widely in physical features, complexion and temperament. Without the admixture of other races, Negroes from these areas would naturally develop many differences over the centuries. It bears repeating that the color black absorbs as much heat as it radiates, and the people with the blackest shin evolved in the jungle belt where temperatures remain pretty much at body heat.

The skin is more than just nature's answer to cellophane for wrapping up flesh and bones. It is the body's most intricate organ. Its pigment protects the tissues and nerves of the body against the destructive effects of the sun's short wavelengths. Blond people have little or no protective pigment because they evolved in the misty climate of northern Europe where the sun's rays are weak. Tobacco and cotton grow in the sun and the sun kills white people if they get too much of it. It gives them skin cancers, for one thing. Negroes do not get skin cancers and the sun doesn't kill them. (However, in the great deserts, where the sun is hottest, the natives have a deep tan or olive complexion, with enough pigment for protection but light enough to reflect most of the heat.)

But there were racial mixtures. Proximity produces cross pollenation to some extent, and there was some racial mixing before the Africans arrived here. The Moors had long controlled the East African slave trade and had even converted some Negroes to Mohammedanism. It was apparent to some observers here that slaves brought from Madascar and Zanzibar included some that had Moorish physical characteristics; and as all slaves were at the mercy of their unscrupulous captors before they were shipped out, some of their children born en-route or shortly after arrival must have been of mixed raced. How many, it would be impossible to guess.

Some other figures on Chart No.4 ought to prove interesting also. The average of mulattoes to the total Negro population of the eleven seceding Southern states is 11.4%, while the average for all the Northern states and territories is 39%! The percentage runs as high as 65% in Minnesota and New Hampshire, and only in New York and New Jersey does it run less than 20%. Such an enormous difference between the two sections must prove that there was less race mixing in the South than in the North however it may have been carried on. The truth should be sufficiently evident to explode popular notions of every young Massa sneaking into the slave cabins at night, and of every old Massa surrounding himself with dark skinned, sloe-eyed beauties while being waited on by servants who were his own offspring.

As a certain late lamented poet might have put it: Facts are more useful but fiction's more juice-ful.

CHAPTER X:

COMPROMISES AND CONCESSIONS

Originally, the two colonies of Massachusetts and Virginia formed the foci of an ellipse which expanded but kept its well balanced proportions until the Revolutionary War. Until then, the Thirteen Colonies were a naturally cohesive combination of political entities united by the same grievances against the Mother Country, although only loosely held together by the Articles of Confederation; but when delegates from the colonies met after the war, and began to set down on paper some rules for a more effective central government, serious differences in ideas and interests became apparent. Some wanted a strong central government, some even wanted a monarchy; others wanted maximum sovereignty for the states. Obviously, compromises had to be reached through concessions. It took a master of diplomacy to accomplish them, and that is why James Madison is known as the Father of the Constitution. But all the concessions were not wise. The beautifully proportioned ellipse was changing shape.

Sectional deviations of interest had always existed but up until the war, the total population of the seven Northern colonies about equalled that of the six Southern colonies, and in 1790 the nation's population center was 23 miles east of Baltimore. Virginia, oldest, richest and most powerful of the colonies, had more than twice as many people as New York, 72% more than Pennsylvania, and 57% more than Massachusetts; but Massachusetts had more white people than Virginia and, Pennsylvania almost as many. The difference was in the growing Negro population of the South, but it was the white population that would affect the political balance. Slaves, having no vote, were counted only three-fifths their number in establishing representation in Congress.

After 1790, the ellipse began to bulge disproportionately westward. The Northwest Territory conquered by George Rogers Clark, was an enormous area from which eventually a half dozen states would be carved out. Within the next 70 years, the nation's total population increased 800% and was 31 1/2 million and the population center had shifted 300 miles to the west. New York's population had grown by 1140% and was 2 1/2 times that of Virginia. Millions of immigrants from many countries had entered the United States, the Europeans settling in the North and West, the Africans in the South as slaves. The total Negro population had increased to 4 1/2 million with fewer than 1/4 million in the Northern states. By 1860, 21 new states had come into the Union but only nine were Southern. The ellipse was gone.

The happy balance was no more. In 1860, the 19 Northern states had a population of 18,887,500 whites and 240,000 Negroes. The 15 Southern states had a population of 8,038,700 whites and 4,201,700 Negroes. This figures out to be one-and-one-third times as many people in the North as in the South, or two-and-one-third times as many whites. The South, which had furnished most of the political leadership was losing its dominant position. The North, including the new western states, now had 38 votes in the Senate to the South's 30. In the House, the disparity was perhaps even worse because sections of the Southern states bordering on Northern states sent representatives to Congress who were not altogether in sympathy with the interests of tobacco and cotton growers.

But long before the addition of the new states had upset the sectional balance, some far-seeing statesmen were aware that tragedy was in the making. There was a fundamental weakness in the Union, a built-in stress that would eventually burst the nation at its seams. A fatal mistake had been made at the Constitutional Convention of 1787. Among other proposals, Virginia had offered an amendment that would require a two-thirds vote for Congress to enact laws regulating commerce and navigation including levying import duties. With most of the manufacturing in the North, and production of raw materials in the South, especially cotton for the North's all-important textile industry, tariffs needed a careful balancing to prevent a hardship on one section or the other.

A high impost on manufactured articles would depress prices for what the South had to sell. Taxation without representation was one cause of the Revolution and ample justification in the minds of most Americans; but what is the difference between being taxed without a vote, and being taxed when your vote is always nullified by an overwhelming majority? A lot of history depended on the adoption or rejection of Virginia's amendment. George Mason said, "The effect of a provision to pass commercial laws by a simple majority would be to deliver the South bound hand and foot to the eastern (New England) states."

There was much opposition to the amendment and, for the sake of securing adoption of the Constitution, James Madison used his expert diplomacy to the end that Virginia finally conceded the point; but George Mason refused to sign the document to which he had contributed so much. He deserves to be better known today. He was the most farsighted of all the members of the Convention.

Other Southerners felt as Mason did, and in Virginia Patrick Henry was the most vocal of the opponents of the Constitution. He predicted that there would be sectional dissent and fratricidal strife. In the end, Virginia voted for adoption by a small margin, and with the proviso that ratification could be rescinded whenever the powers granted to the Union should be perverted to the injury or oppression of the Old Dominion. This seemed at the time like sufficient protection, and the same proviso was insisted upon by several other states.[1]

CHAPTER XI:

ENCIRCLEMENT

Did the Northern industrialists want a war to end slavery? No, not to end slavery, but to end the South or, put more accurately, they wanted an end to Southern power and influence in the Nation. They, or those members of the industrialist clique who dominated the Republican Party then, were determined to dominate the country by whatever means; but slavery was too profitable for it to be ended until they could bring off their grandiose plan of domination. There was no way they could have both the profits of slavery AND domination of the nation; and domination was far more important. Forcing an end to slavery was the handiest method of destroying the South.

Many people will not accept the idea that any man or group of men have ever plotted or ever would plot to take over absolute control of the United States, but they forget that men have risked and lost life and fortune trying to gain control of countries that had nothing but debts and poverty. Men with the power urge have been present everywhere and at all times, ready to seize opportunity when it presented itself. Why would men of boundless ambition pass up this richest of all prizes? They didn't pass it up, and their plans succeeded.

Big things were happening and getting bigger as the 19th century went into its second quarter, making big changes in the lives and thoughts of people. Southern planters were getting rich and enjoying a glamorous social life by raising cotton for Northern, British and European mills to weave into fabrics that were clothing the world; and tobacco was delighting the world's smokers, chewers and takers of snuff. Their slaves too were "gettin' fat or a little fatter on buckwheat cakes and Injun batter". Northern mill owners were getting rich too, and politically, even socially, ambitious. Their humming mills were returning handsome profits, and their ships were putting plenty of jingle from the jungle into their pockets; but their mill hands were not becoming very obese on the wages doled out to them at the end of each six fourteen-hour days. And life for the owner and his employees alike in the dingy offices and shops amid a forest of smoke stacks lacked something of the glamorous. So it seemed, at least, to the Southerner in the pastoral environment of his plantation home.[1]

It has often been said in the South that it was envy that first set fire to the New England conscience and made it sensitive to the evils of slavery, but that is a shallow observation. There is always envy where riches and social position are concerned, but envy itself would not justify an expensive war. To a hardheaded business man, especially a New England business man, there had to be a practical purpose in everything. Envy, merely as a state of mind, was a waste of time and therefore a sin, but when it was harnessed to something practical, it could be fitted out with the vestments of a righteous cause. A good deal of abolitionist propaganda was, deliberately or otherwise, designed to arouse envy of the "indolent" Southern planter enjoying luxuries derived from oppressing slave workers. Lincoln's off quoted "you make the bread and I'll eat it" is a good example.

Westward expansion was accomplished mostly by Southerners. It was Thomas Jefferson and James Monroe who were responsible for the Louisiana Purchase (New Englanders were against it) and it was Meriwether Lewis and William Clark who explored it. All four were Virginians. It was North Carolina's James K. Polk who was responsible for the acquisition of Texas, New Mexico, Arizona and California; Virginia's Winfield Scott and Zachary Taylor who led U.S. forces to victory against Santa-Anna, and Stephen F. Austin and Sam Houston who founded Texas. Edward Bates, Lincoln's Attorney General was a Virginian before he became a Missourian, and so was Stevens Thomas Mason, first governor of the state of Michigan.

As new Western areas were peopled and became new states, though their citizens were drawn mostly from the South, they had few economic reasons for political alignment with the Southern states. Of those that did, Kentucky, Missouri and Tennessee had large areas where neither tobacco or cotton was a major crop. Delaware and Maryland were similarly situated, making the South weak in several places along its perimeter. The geographic limits of tobacco and cotton had been reached. Negro labor, neither slave nor free, was wanted or needed in the new West, and slavery had become a sectional institution.

But these new Western states were agricultural, not industrial. Why weren't they in sympathy with the South? They likewise had a one-crop economy. Why didn't they also need Negro slave labor?

The difference was that the one-crop economy of the West was wheat, and in the production of wheat there were not the many manual operations required in the production of cotton or tobacco. The growing and processing of wheat was adapted to the mechanization of the times. Instead of Negro labor, Western farmers could more efficiently employ Cyrus McCormick's "Virginia Reaper", ironically another contribution from the Old Dominion to the Union.

Though originally Southerners, the people of the West, busy fighting the forces of nature and the forces of the Indians, soon forgot their origins and traditions. When ties to the past become tenuous, old fallacies can be sold as new truths. The West began to look toward the Northeast and listen to Northern propaganda.

War is a chancy thing and something to be avoided if a purpose can be attained without it. Jefferson Davis and other conservative Southerners knew that secession was likely to bring on war and they strove to avoid it. They only succeeded in postponing it, and the odds would have been in favor of the South if it had come earlier. Encirclement would not have been so complete.

The political base was shifting. As the West grew and the probability of a natural alliance with the Northeast was perceived, the industrial group saw conditions ripe for acquiring control. Opportunity had been put into their hands. Would men with the opportunity and capability of exploiting a great advantage decline to do so? Have men in any country at any time ever?

The Northern states were freeing their slaves (or selling them South) and the new Western states were not adopting slavery. Therefore, with slavery a geographical institution, exclusively Southern, the abolitionists in attacking slavery, were attacking the South. Why shouldn't the industrialists encourage them? The new states were choosing to be "free soil", but for an alliance with the Northeast it was necessary for them to be anti-slavery, violently anti-slavery, and the abolitionist propaganda could make them so. The Western pioneers could be convinced that their political and economic interests were identical to those of the Northeasterners, and they could be aroused into sharing the emotional attitude of New England abolitionists. They could be convinced that expanding slavery would rob the honest, hard working white Northern and Western workers of their daily bread. They could be sold the whole war party package: that the South was trying to dominate the nation and run the government for the benefit of a fat slaveholding oligarchy. It would be easy to make them hate people they didn't know but who had more than they did.

Lincoln's "House divided" speech convinced many that the nation could not exist "half slave and half free", though Lincoln didn't mention that the "slave" portion of the country was one-third or less, not half by any means; nor did he explain how two-thirds of the nation could be forced by one-third into supplanting free labor with slaves; but mathematical accuracy is apt to spoil emotional political appeals. People willingly accepted as fact that soon Negro slaves would be taking the jobs of white workers unless something drastic was done about it. Seward's "Irrepressible conflict" speech that followed soon afterward hammered home the same point. The North was breathing war.

These "scare tactics" threatened the bread on the table which, in many places in the West was not too secure at best. A threat to one's means of making a living is still a good tactic today, even with all the cushioning provided by law and federal appropriations. In the days when the nation was entirely without anything but voluntary charity for those who couldn't find work, the instinct of self- preservation was keener.

CHAPTER XII:

LOP-SIDED LEGISLATION

So here was an established Southern leadership, rich and
still growing richer, but founded on a narrowing base; while
across the great divide made famous by Mason and Dixon,
was a competitive group growing newly rich on the expanding base of new states. It was inevitable that this oncoming
group would have aspirations for leadership and exploit
their opportunities to the fullest; and it needed no great genius to see the most feasible way of gratifying their ambitions.

The spirits that whisper in the ears of aspiring despots were
fairly shouting at the emerging industrialists, "Destroy the
prosperity of the old group and make the South completely
dependent upon the North". It was obvious that slavery, in
which the South had such a huge investment, could not be
ended instantly as the abolitionists demanded, by any
peaceful means. Less obvious was the fact that the Northern industrial bloc, the so-called "War Party" didn't want
slavery ended peacefully. That would leave too much power
in the hands of the Southern governing class. Remnant
groups of Federalists, the National Republicans and Northern Whigs that had been thrown out of power half a century
before, would do anything to unseat the Democrats and control the country themselves.

It is amazing that so many people still do not see how impossible instant emancipation would have been, and how
ridiculous the abolitionist position really was. No one
seems to have sat down with a pencil and used a little
fourth grade arithmetic. In 1860, the Industrial Revolution
was less than 100 years old, and the present sharp delin-
eation between capital and labor had not completely
emerged. A plantation was all capital. The slaves were capital. They represented a large part of the total investment
and were collateral for loans. In 1860, the total value of real
estate in Alabama was estimated at $235,550,000, while the
total value of personal property and slaves was estimated at

$557,000,000 over twice as much. Plantations, like all business enterprises, operated on borrowed money. Sudden emancipation would have wiped out collateral for many millions in loans, and have been an instant disaster for slave and master both. Under any plan, converting slaves from capital to labor would have been a problem of finance.[1]

Compare instant emancipation with an instant crash of the Stock Market. On "Black Friday", October 29, 1929, an estimated 15 billions of dollars worth of capital evaporated (not exactly instantly but before the end of the year) causing one of the worst depressions the country ever had. The total population of the country in 1929 was 120 million and the crash meant a loss of $125 for each man, woman and child. In 1860, with a population of 12 million in the South, a two billion dollar loss of capital would have meant a loss of $166 for each man, woman and child, Negroes included; but as almost all of the assets were held by whites, the total per capita loss would have been $266, more than double that of the 1929 crash.[2]

For another perspective: suppose the federal government suddenly confiscated all farm machinery without compensation to the owners, and then said, "Now you must pay rent for whatever equipment you need, but you will also have to keep up payments on the notes and mortgages you executed when you bought the equipment that was confiscated". How could a farmer get a crop started? Or a bank collect its loans? How could anyone hire any help, or a farm hand earn a dollar for something to eat?

With instant emancipation, what would have happened to the freed slaves? They had no property or any reserves, and who would have any money to pay them wages? These considerations didn't seem to bother the abolitionists. For them, slavery had to be destroyed even if the Negro was destroyed too.

It would help to consider here the question of exactly how the abolitionists appraised their own efforts. What did they actually think they were accomplishing? Or did they ever pause, and think, and ask themselves what logical results could be expected to flow from their rantings and ravings?

Did they think they could intimidate the slaveholders into setting free all their slaves on one and the same day? Did they think that if they could induce the slaves to rise up and slaughter their masters (and their masters' families) that everything in the South would be sweetness and light for the ex-slaves and for the nation?

What, especially, did they think they were accomplishing via the "underground railroad"? How many, or what percentage of the slave population did they think could be set free that way? How much of that sort of thing would the Northern people have tolerated? How many freed slaves did the abolitionists think they could establish in the North before people there rose up and put an end to the abolitionists themselves?

It would be easy to say that their efforts were just demonstrations to dramatize the problem and convince the nation that pressure should be put on the slave owners to come to terms with their slaves, set them free (instantly, all on the same day?) employ them and pay them wages (with what?); but such a comfortable attitude toward the abolition movement would have to deny a lot of facts.

There seemed no logic whatever in the movement, no practical goal in anybody's mind, no reasoned out and intelligently directed plan. The whole thing was a classic example of fanaticism run wild, another blind extermination urge, a craze to destroy all the infidels, all the witches, all the forces of evil, a wave of mass insanity that swept the land. History records a number of such.

The big behind-the-scenes Northern industrialists with their enormous financial resources were making political decisions, and these hard-headed people weren't playing for pumpkin seeds. They were out to win more enormous wealth and power, and the 1860 census shows how the balance was shaping up. The 15 states in the Southern bloc were Alabama, Arkansas, Delaware, Florida, Georgia, Kentucky, Louisiana, Maryland, Mississippi, Missouri, North Carolina, South Carolina, Tennessee, Texas and Virginia (including what is now West Virginia).

These 15 states comprised all the land in the country where Negro labor could be used profitably in large numbers and to better advantage than white labor. The South had reached its peak of expansion. There were 8 million white people and 4 1/2 million Negroes, and nowhere could the South look for additional political strength. In the North there were 19 million white people and 1/4 million Negroes and a vast area of undeveloped territory which was rapidly being settled with people whose economic interests would not be with the South. Against such odds, the South could not hope to hold its own within the Union. On every issue, the South was being and would continue to be outvoted, especially on commercial regulations. Paying high prices for what it bought and getting low prices for what it sold would have brought the South completely under the domination of the North, the "North" really being the rest of the country.

It was to head off this kind of lop-sided legislation that the two-thirds majority requirement for enacting laws regulating commerce was proposed at the Constitutional Convention; and for the same reason the doctrine of "Concurrent Majority" was sponsored by John C. Calhoun. This doctrine would have permitted any state or group of states to protect themselves by a veto power over measures passed by a simple majority if such measures proved of special disadvantage to the minority state or states.

Calhoun's doctrine had merit and, accepted in good faith by the majority, it could have averted the war. It would have been hard to administer, but what plan, under the circumstances, wouldn't have been? The trouble was that it had to be adopted by the majority and the majority was not about to limit its power by approving a substitute for the two-thirds rule. It became known as "Nullification" and was bitterly opposed by Andrew Jackson. But no one offered anything better.

The attitude of the South has never been well understood because the insistence of the abolitionists upon instant and unconditional emancipation forced the South to defend slavery whereas the South most wanted an end to it. No practical plan for ending slavery was being proposed by anybody, perhaps because there was none. Cool heads might have worked out a plan for some kind of gradual emancipation which could have been preparation for the impact of farm machinery later on; but there could be few cool heads in the climate created by radical, fanatical abolition.

In any discussion of freedom for the slaves, questions came up for which there was no precedent to provide an answer. What would Negroes do with new found freedom if it wre given to large numbers at one time? Could they use it wisely without advance preparation, and what kind of advance preparation could be devised? Would they show up for work as usual, come back to the same plantations? Would labor be available when needed to start a crop, cultivate it, harvest it? Would free Negroes take care of their old and sick or let them become public charges?

Would Negroes do better work as free workers than they did as slaves? If so, would there be a surplus of labor, with layoffs and idle workers? On the other hand, if free labor proved LESS efficient than slave labor (and here is the question that must have been in the minds of responsible Southerners for a long time) and more expensive, and if the cost of cotton and tobacco production rose to the point where the South had to price itself out of the world market, what would happen? The answer is obvious. Mill owners and tobacco buyers in the North and those in Britain and Europe would buy from the cheapest source, from Egypt, for instance for cotton, from the Spanish and Portugese colonies for tobacco, places where slave labor was used. Nowhere was either cotton or tobacco raised by free labor. Slavery would increase in foreign countries, supported by our own industry, while the South, and especially the Southern Negroes starved, and a worse than zero accomplishment for the abolitionists would result.

In any event, converting the entire economic system in the South from slavery to free labor would be taking a giant step into the unknown. It would have been a multi-billion dollar gamble too awesome to be undertaken without better assurance of success than could be provided at the time. Solution to the problem of slavery could have been best accomplished by abolition of the abolitionists, allowing patience and sincerity to await what time had to offer. And time had a lot to offer, and not far off.

CHAPTER XIII:

WAR CLIMATE

The climax toward which all events were moving was war, and all essentials were present: (1) an established agricultural class furnishing most of the military and political leadership, rich but at the peak of its power; (2) a new industrial class gaining wealth and political influence, ambitious for more of both, allied with political groups out of office for a long time and willing to do anything to regain power; (3) a violently emotional issue promoted by fanatical crusaders, to stir the people; (4) a president who surpassed all previous presidents in lust for power, who had devoted all his adult years to his ambition.

That the two classes, agricultural and industrial, were geographically sectional lessened chances for mutual understanding. That there were fabulous opportunities opening up for the industrial class to gain power fired the ambitions of the unscrupulous to the point of recklessness. But the industrialists did not originate the abolition crusade. That developed coincidentally and played into their hands as conflicting interests moved the two sections toward confrontation. The abolitionists got going on their own. It might not be polite to say that they were the spiritual descendants of the Salem witch hunters of 150 years before, but they were certainly a product of fanaticism generated in New England. During the two decades before the war, with the aid of clergy and politicians, the abolitionists enjoyed wide public support. Their great service to the "War Party" was in providing an emotional issue that would prepare the people psychologically for war.

The way always has to be prepared in advance for possible use of force, so that if other means fail to accomplish the desired objective the public will support extreme measures. Labor negotiations, for instance, are always preceded by charges against employers to stir the union members to support a strike if offers are rejected. Among nations today that is called "negotiating from a position of strength", and the nations that make the most use of it cry "foul!" when others use it. It is obvious however, that a nation that does not negotiate from a position of strength stands little chance of carrying an important point.

The abolitionists did an energetic job of creating a war climate. They had been learning the techniques a long time. They charged the atmosphere with the most explosive of gases, and hurled at the South an unprecedented volume of vituperation in the most livid language. Writers and orators, professionals and amateur, lay and clerical loaned their talents to the effort. Webster's dictionary was torn to shreds in a frantic search for denunciatory words and phrases. The Bible and classical literature were scoured for similes, syllogisms, symbolisms, allegories, metaphors plain and mixed, and every device of rhetoric. Seemingly only the undecipherable Linear B inscriptions were left unscathed in the quest for maledictions to heap upon the collective head of Southern slaveholders. The worst horrors of fact and fiction described by ancient and current writers were cited as examples of minor wrong doing compared to the fiendish evil of indolent, arrogant, haughty, prejudiced, soul-destroying Southerners; and still the abolitionists suffered from a sense of frustration at their inadequacy to express sufficiently their holy hatred for slavery and slave owners. The period ought to be known to history as "The Age of Invective".

War is not caused by hatred. It is the other way round. Hatred is manufactured, like munitions, as a necessary instrument of war. War is caused by a conflict of selfish interests; the hatred between the warring parties seems usually to have nothing to do with the real causes of war. The men actually called on to do the fighting do not usually hate each other, nor do they usually have any clear notion of the real causes of the war they are fighting, certainly not clear enough to induce them to risk their lives in battle, but they must be given something to hate, some dragon to kill, some personal glory to win or, for mercenaries, opportunity for looting. The abolitionists were giving the future musket carriers an image that could be hated with religious zeal, an "indolent aristocrat", a leering fiend who tortured helpless slaves and grew rich on profits his slaves earned for him while he sipped his juleps.

The two words "indolent" and "aristocrat" were linked in holy wordlock, like "damyankee". Seldom was one heard without the other. The trouble with the holy hatred the abolitionists generated was that, while it fired the Northerners with zeal, it also fired the Southerners with at least as much counter-zeal. The spirit of Confederate troops often more than offset a disparity in numbers. But the image of the slaveholder lolling in luxury also enlisted the services of the "Green Eyed Monster". To righteous indignation, the abolitionists had added envy. Envy and hate are old companions that have never failed to help each other out. These were the two that inspired the widespread pillaging that made an ineradicable black mark on the record of Northern troops, more especially the foreign troops recruited abroad who had no feeling for the people on either side. Some men, of course, justified their pillaging on the theory that the slaveholder's property was wrongfully acquired and it was therefore no sin to take it away from him. That theory is as old as theivery.

Oliver Wendell Holmes, later Chief Justice of the Supreme Court, was a young lieutenant in the Union Army at the Battle of Fredericksburg and was horrified at the pillaging and destructive vandalism of drunken Northern troops who made bonfires in the streets fueled with furniture taken from private residences. The "White House" at West Point, Virginia, home of Martha Washington before her marriage to the "Father of our Country" was maliciously burned, and Sherwood Forest, the 36 room mansion that belonged to John Tyler still stands only because a heroic Negro maid pulled the burning straw from under a table where it had been set, but there are still deep scars made by gun butts on the front door and sabre slashes on the walls and portraits. These are only three out of many wanton examples that occurred. They happen in all wars, but this one was "for preservation" of the Union,- as if war could preserve anything.[1]

The effect of abolition efforts on Southern sentiment is well illustrated by Northern reaction to John Brown's raid on the United States armory at Harper's Ferry. Brown and his band had shortly before taken five poor Kansas farmers from the midst of their families, murdered them and mutilated their bodies. These farmers had nothing to do with slavery or politics in any way. In Virginia, Brown or his men shot a free Negro named Heywood Shepherd, a B & O Railroad porter. They left him lying in the road twelve hours until he died, and ignored his pleas for water.

To the people of the South, these were the acts of a mad dog killer, but when Brown was captured, a surge of sympathetic sentiment swept the North to the dismay and chagrin of many anti-secession Southerners. The South was horrified when Phillips Brooks said that John Brown "had gilded (the Potomac River) with the eternal brightness of his glorious deed" and Ralph Waldo Emerson said Brown "would make the gallows glorious like the Cross". Thomas Wentworth Higginson of Boston was interested in a plot to kidnap Governor Wise of Virginia and hold him hostage for Brown. These do not sound like men who wanted the Union preserved. They were obviously declaring war upon the South, a war of extermination. Many anti-secessionists were convinced that there was no longer any hope of justice for the South within the Union. Now, 120 years afterward with all the facts known and unquestioned, why is Harper's Ferry maintained as a sacred memorial to the mad man John Brown?

CHAPTER XIV:

THE FIRST SHOT

In addition to a good war climate, one thing a nation needs before launching itself into a war is a strong political position built up by a clever arrangement of preliminary events. Without that a nation could lose support of other nations and of elements within itself if the war proved longer than expected, and collapse under the strain of furnishing men and supplies and when people have to go without necessities. Lincoln was a smart politician.

He had been able to figure out where he wanted to go and how to get there. He kept himself aloof from too close an identification with any particular group or cause until he found out which one was going to be the dominant political force in the country. Being from Illinois was an advantage. Illinois was a divided state. Its Northern portion was abolitionist in sentiment, its lower portion, if not pro-Southern, was at least moderate, prone to compromise. Lincoln talked in both directions on the slavery issue, admitting the constitutionality of slavery but denouncing it for brutality, thereby appealing to both sections. By observing their reactions he could gauge which was gaining strength. A good politician looks ahead.

Lincoln was quick to see a "turn", and was the first to make an appeal for support from a group of immigrants. He purchased the first German language newspaper published in this country. (Later he would import German mercenaries just as George III had done four score and seven years before.) Lincoln kept his center of gravity until he saw that the industrialists were definitely in the ascendancy, then he shifted his weight accordingly.[1]

Many people will not accept the charge that Lincoln was the tool of the unscrupulous plotters and planners for the domination of the country. Trained from childhood on the stories that reflected a saintly image upon Lincoln, they hesitate to discard their early dreams, which is understandable, but the facts have been shouting loud enough and for a long enough time at least to arouse serious questions even in the minds of his most ardent admirers. Even in the South, Lincoln's part in bringing on the conflict does not seem to be fully appreciated. American history is not a required subject in most colleges, and there are many phases that cannot be adequately presented to immature students in elementary and secondary schools. Most people, even Southerners, are willing to concede that Lincoln was a "good" man, that his actions were inspired by a deep concern for "human rights" and were not politically inspired; that he could not prevent the war, and that if he had lived, the horrors of reconstruction would not have occurred. What were Lincoln's motives?

Did he want the South destroyed? No, he just wanted to be president. He had the power urge, the old, old lust for empire that drove Xerxes, Alexander, Caesar, Alaric, William I, Genghis Khan, Napoleon, Hitler, Lenin and many, many more, but which is not supposed to be any part of an American politician's make-up. How good or bad was Lincoln? Only with a deaf ear to what he said, and a keen eye on what he did, can one gauge his character accurately. He was an expert in the use of words and phrases and classical quotations as well as ribald anecdotes, and the meanings of these was often deliberately obscure or ambiguous so that they might fit whatever action he chose to take later as expedience dictated. Flexible? Or shifty? But clever.

The Northern people never realized that Lincoln was elected to get a war going, but Southern leaders, whose instincts for self preservation made them more sensitive to trends, saw no other answer to the question of why he was nominated. They foresaw that his election would mean the end of Southern political freedom and economic independence, and the beginning of Southern subordination to Northern industrial interests, the hard core of which had adopted Lincoln as its "front man".

That Lincoln, or any other ambitious political leader, wanted war can always be challenged because, with each, war was only a means to an end, or the inevitable result of their efforts to accomplish certain results. If the North could have achieved complete domination of the country without war, there would have been no war. If the South had been willing to submit peacefully to being outvoted on every issue, burdened with excessive taxes through exorbitant tariffs, and ruined financially by disruption of their economic and social system, everything would have been just fine,- for the North. It can therefore be said that it was not war that Lincoln was planning, but how to accomplish the objectives of the Northern economic interests. However, it was obvious that Southerners would fight for their rights as any self-respecting people would, and that the program of the industrial clique could not be carried out except by coercion. As the screws were tightened, the only question was, at what point would the South wrench free? They could not afford to wait until they were utterly unable to resist.

Lincoln was strictly a party politician and a sectional president. It has been remarked that in politics, nothing happens by accident. It is also observable that the only commitments sacred to a party politician are those made to other politicians. Commitments made to the public mean little. The public forgets, but not politicians. Violation of an intrapolitical agreement means political death. Lincoln was a Republican, and the Republican Party at that time was in the hands of a determined group of politically shrewd, economically powerful, morally unscrupulous men.

Many Southerners opposed secession, not on moral or constitutional grounds, but because they thought it was not the wisest means of trying to obtain Southern rights, and they did not want to sever themselves from the Union that their fathers and grandfathers had brought into being. The question, though, was not one of being for or against the Union. People in the South were willing to let the Northern people have their Union. The North had no right to force the South to remain in it. The South wanted a Union of its own.

But people in the Northern states were being whipped into

an emotional frenzy by the aggressive, well financed abolitionists and were becoming implacably hostile. Tariffs,
pushed through by Northern majorities, were strangling the
South. Lincoln, in a pre-election speech had made an overt
threat to the South, using the words, "we will force you". As
the dividing lines were being drawn, people were being com-
pelled to take up a position on one side or the other. The
question was which group of states, which Union, deserved
one's loyalty.[1]

For a proper perspective, it is important to remember that
at no time did the people of the South or their leaders have
any aggressive designs on the North, or any desire to destroy the Union. Without the bitter feeling generated by the
abolitionists, it might have been possible for all to see the
necessity of a two-thirds rule giving the South enough voting strength to block oppressive taxation, and the conflict
could have been averted. Jefferson Davis, as president of
the Confederacy said, "All we want is to be let alone". The
South was willing to let the North alone.[2]

The difference in attitude between the two sections toward
the Union is illustrated by a confrontation years before the
war between Andrew Jackson and John C. Calhoun, both
South Carolinians but bitter enemies. At a banquet, Jackson proposed a toast, with a glare at Calhoun, "To the
UNION!" Then Calhoun, with a return glare at Jackson,
proposed, "To the Union! Next to our liberties, most dear!"

Conditions in the 1860's were screaming for negotiation,
concession, compromise, but during his campaign for election, Lincoln made no effort to win over the South. He knew
he would get few votes there, and didn't want to risk losing
any in the North by appearing too weak, perhaps.

It was a foregone conclusion that, with sectional feeling at
such high pitch, some or all of the Southern states would secede if Lincoln was elected. Most thinking people hoped
that this would not bring on a war, but there were some who
thought it would have to come, and some who actually
wanted war. But things did not happen as they were appar-

ently expected to. They never do.

Lincoln's election became known to all early in November 1860, and on December 20, South Carolina seceded, hoisted the Palmetto Flag, and became an independent nation, but carefully avoided making any move that might be construed as an act of war. Major Robert Anderson with a force of 86 men and officers, was at Fort Moultrie, opposite Fort Sumter. He was instructed by President Buchanan not to make any move that could be construed as hostile. Buchanan was being advised by some to re-inforce the small garrison and by others to withdraw it. He temporized. What else could he do? He was holding a bear by the tail, waiting for his successor to take over, not knowing what Lincoln's plans were and no way of finding out, as the two were political enemies.

South Carolina sent envoys to negotiate for federal property but they couldn't see the president. Buchanan was urged to declare that force would not be used but he declared that such decisions were up to Congress. Anderson, charged with defending his small force and U.S. property, fearful of attack and unable to get specific instructions, finally occupied Fort Sumter after making careful, secret plans. There, he had a better chance of surviving an attack; but this was an act of war and in violation of his instructions. It infuriated South Carolinians. Without awaiting result of negotiations and Buchanan's decision whether to reinforce or withdraw Anderson, Governor Pickens, in retaliation, ordered other U.S. government property seized, also an act of war, but both sides were then even. However, General Winfield Scott, after wheedling approval out of the President, loaded ammunition, supplies and 200 soldiers into the steamer "Star of the West" and sent it secretly to Fort Sumter. The secret got out, and on January 9, flying the U.S.Flag but concealing the troops below deck, the ship steamed up the narrow channel toward the fort and was fired on by a shore battery. Forced to turn about, the "Star of the West" steamed back to New Yourk with a dent in her bow from a Southern cannon ball.[1]

This was the first shot of the war. The flag had been fired on, but nobody in the North rose up in arms. Those who had been screaming for war screamed a little louder and those who had been urging peace urged a little more fervently, but nothing really happened. (Actually, the flag had been fired on before that, at Harper's Ferry, by John Brown, but no Northern hand was raised against him.)

The reason this "first shot" did not start the war was that President Buchanan was determined that there would be no bloodshed during his administration, though he refused to order Anderson back into Fort Moultrie. Whether or not that would have done any good is a matter for speculation.

On the same day as the "Star of the West" incident, Mississippi seceded, and by February 1, five other states had gone out: Florida, Alabama, Georgia, Louisiana and Texas,- Texas! that had so recently fought a desperate war of liberation from the tyrant Santa-Anna, and had voted enthusiastically to join the Union only 16 years before! The seven states formed themselves into the Confederate States of America, with its capital at Montgomery, Alabama, elected Jefferson Davis "The Voice of the South" as its president, adopted the "Stars-and-Bars" as its official flag, and sent delegates to Washington hoping for a constructive conference.[2]

Lincoln was innaugurated on March 4, and in the meantime had given no indication of how he would deal with the crisis, nor did he do so for more than a month afterward. It may be that he and the Northern War Party were taken by surprise by the calmness with which secession was being greeted even by the most rabid abolitionists. Even Horace Greely urged that the cotton states be allowed to "go in peace", and Wendell Phillips said, "Now the South will no longer hate the North" (Sic!) But Phillips did say that now the two nations could carry on a profitable trade. He saw that the two sections complemented each other, that the North could now have its high tariff on manufactured articles and low tariff on raw materials, while the South could have just the reverse. He failed to see, though, that this was not what the industrialists wanted. They wanted a captive South that could be held in subjection and exploited.[1]

Other abolitionists also welcomed Southern secession. Frederick Douglass said that now a man as brave as William Walker could arise and invade the South with a thousand men (Sic!), raise the banner of freedom and attract as many as 60,000 followers to force Southern slaveholders to release their bondsmen. He never thought about a black William Walker and a band of Negro filibusters to make war on African slave nations and force them out of the business of selling their own people into slavery, most of which was far worse than the kind that existed here. But Douglass was not unique in this.[2]

The universal failure to understand the fundamentals of the slavery problem is astounding, and current estimates of what it would take to subdue the South now seem inexcusable except that fanatics build themselves into an idea so thoroughly that they can't come into contact with any other idea. Although Douglass' ideas seem childish, he at least seemed to be trying to express the more realistic thought that it would be more in conformity with the Constitution to make war upon the South as a foreign nation than to fight states that were still in the Union; and he was only 20% worse than Lincoln in his estimate of the manpower needed for the job for which Lincoln called up 75,000 men for three months service, though Lincoln must have intended these only "for openers".

But here was a war all set up and nobody was coming to it. If the casual reaction of the abolitionists toward secession spread and took hold of the people, men's minds might turn away from the prospect of war. It seems to have required considerable political skill to prevent an unexpected peace from descending upon the land. Eight Southern states had not seceded and did not want to secede: Arkansas, Delaware, Kentucky, Maryland, Missouri, North Carolina, Tennessee and Virginia. They were all anxious to exert their good offices to bring about a peaceful solution. There were many alternatives to war, many possibilities that had never been explored.

This was a moment for statesmanship. The big question in everybody's mind was, "Will Lincoln negotiate or resort to coercion?" What could be lost by negotiating? Right across the river was Virginia, her leaders willing to exert all their talents in the cause of Union and peace with justice. The Union was the product of Virginia's Washington and Madison, the Constitution a product of Virginia's Mason and Jefferson.[1] It was unthinkable that their efforts should now prove to be all in vain, that the land they loved and strove so hard to safeguard with constitutional guarantees should be ravaged by a war of invasion. Some friends did get to see Lincoln and urge against the use of force, but the only concern he showed was for federal revenues.[2]

It is unrealistic to believe that Lincoln, skilled politician that he was, would have found it impossible to use his talents for peace. One simple device might have been a prompt post-election speech offering to discuss proposals from the South. This might have brought down to half speed the rush toward secession, and a formula for peaceful co-existence might have been worked out. But Lincoln made no move. He never tried for peace. Why? There seems but one answer: he knew that there was no peaceful way the ambitious industrial clique could carry out its program for subjugation of the South.

During that pleasant springtime of 1861, when warm blood was flowing in young veins and hopes of a happy future glowing in the hearts of young lovers, wouldn't a man of good will, undominated by evil influences, have done his best to prevent the death and devastation of a war in which America would have to lose every battle? Wouldn't a man with malice toward none have made SOME move to keep the reluctant eight Southern states from joining the seven that had already gone out? But Lincoln said nothing, and left the people, South and North, filled with suspense, waiting for his announcement of policy. The country was still a powder keg, and Lincoln knew as well as anyone that whenever there is a powder keg around, somebody is going to drop a match into it, deliberately or accidentally. Was he waiting for somebody else to drop the match so that he could wash his hands of innocent blood as Pilate had done?

He allowed the South Carolinians, and the officials of the newly formed Confederate government to become convinced that Anderson's force would be withdrawn from Fort Sumter. (Swanberg states that Seward, on his own, assured the governor of this, but it is hard to believe that a Secretary of State would proceed in such a sensitive matter without at least tacit approval of the president.)[1] After months of contradictory and confusing official and unofficial statements and rumors, Lincoln had a convoy secretly put together in a plan to provision the fort but with warships standing by to land men and arms if the attempt at provisioning was resisted. Anderson was notified this would take place April 11 or 12. On the night of April 8, a messenger delivered a message to Governor Pickens of South Carolina which was a blunt notification that such an attempt would be made. It was insulting in the extreme. It had no address or signature or other courtesies, and was delivered by a mere clerk who was not authorized to accept a reply. It was exactly the kind of thing certain to arouse anger and suspicion of a trick. Provisions indeed! More likely a fleet of warships ready to blast Charleston and land a full complement of men at the fort![2]

Buchanan had been bumbling and confusing but Lincoln was being insulting and deceitful. If the Confederates waited for these "provisions", they would be at the mercy of an unscrupulous foe, it stood to reason. Three officers were dispatched to the fort to demand, with all military courtesy, that Anderson evacuate Sumter, stipulating that he could take all personal and government property with him and salute his flag with an appropriate number of guns. When Anderson declined, as they knew he would, and expressed his thanks for the generous terms, they informed him of the hour at which bombardment would begin. It was a sad occasion. Anderson had been an instructor at West Point and Beauregard, in command at Charleston, had been his favorite pupil. There was still a warm feeling of friendship and respect between the two. Anderson was a Kentuckian and entirely in sympathy with the South though he could not make the decision to break with the Union.

Lincoln's expedition really did have orders to land provisions only, unless resisted, and then to force reinforcements into the fort. For the purpose, some warships were to be on hand and some tugs, but things got fouled up. The tugs went astray, the biggest warship was diverted elsewhere, and the others could only wait outside the harbor beyond range while the bombardment proceeded. Swanberg speculates that if the Confederates had known the condition of the expedition, they could have delayed action for a few days, keeping the ships at bay until Anderson would have had to evacuate the fort because his food supply was exhausted. Peaceful evacuation might have taken enough tension out of the situation to make room for reason. Maybe so, but Lincoln's insulting message betrayed a deep hatred that would sooner or later have found another match for the powder keg. It is hard to shrug off the significance of that note.

And so Lincoln had played his sleeve card. While the world was waiting for a declaration of his policy, he launched the nation into a war that would destroy fully one-fourth of his country, kill half a million young men and maim a million more. Certainly his actions at this time were those of a man who had long been determined upon war; and what kind of war? He knew full well that almost 100% of the Southern people were of one mind on the fundamental issues. He knew that his actions would be bitterly contested by one-fourth to one-third of the nation's population, and that he would be fighting one-third of the states, yet he treated these states and their people with cold contempt and refused to see their emissaries.

What did he visualize as the results of his decision? He must have known that, against a people as solidly united and determined as the Southern people had proved themselves to be, it would not be a matter of simply sending an expedition to round up a few ring leaders with a fickle following, hang them and establish peace throughout the land. He knew it would have to be a war of extermination. He would have to destroy so many homes, farms, factories, warehouses, mills, railroads, horses, mules, so much food and fodder and kill so many of his fellow Americans that there would not be enough men and material remaining to hold the line against an invasion of overwhelming numbers. This would be the kind of war an alien conqueror would undertake for the subjugation and exploitation of a despised people.

CHAPTER XV:

EXCITING ATMOSPHERE

The "Star of the West" incident had clearly shown that the best way to get a war started was to re-inforce Fort Sumter. The move was an act of war and Lincoln knew it. His cabinet knew it too and with two exceptions (one weak) voted against it; but Lincoln knew that the public wouldn't know it and would consider any act on the part of Southern forces an act of aggression. And this time Lincoln would see to it that the incident was properly exploited as an act of open rebellion against constituted authority. His thinking was politically sound.[1]

News of the attack was accompanied by Lincoln's call for 75,000 men to "put down the rebellion", and it had the desired effect. It blew the bugle and unified the Northern people, whetting their appetite for war; but it also unified the Southern people. It confirmed in the Northern mind that the South was determined upon destroying the Union completely, and it confirmed in the Southern mind what Southerners had long known, that Lincoln had been elected to make war upon them.

Lincoln well knew that in spite of the emotions aroused in the North by the abolitionists, the Northern people would not fight to free the Negroes. There would have to be a better cause and a good slogan to rally the enthusiasm of troops as well as the folks at home. For years he had been selling "Union" as the major issue, and just about all of his speeches emphasized it. The slogan "The Union Must Be Preserved!" caught on and convinced people in the North that they were fighting to prevent complete dissolution of the Union. Somehow secession of the Southern states would make continuation of any kind of union impossible anywhere. Nobody asked why it would, or how you could preserve something by destroying it. That was mob manipulation.

The basis of Lincoln's attitude was that secession had been

carried out by a limited number of Southern leaders and that union could be restored when these people had been captured and punished. Obviously, this was fiction and Lincoln knew it. He could not help but know that secession had been voted overwhelmingly by the people themselves, and it took no great political genius to see that the South was united as few nations have been, though it had just come into being as a nation itself.[1]

Confederate leadership had been criticized for attacking Fort Sumter and giving Lincoln the excuse for launching his invasion, but the attack was not ordered impulsively or for frivolous reasons. All efforts to hold talks and discuss peace had been rebuffed, efforts to pry a declaration of policy out of Lincoln had failed and had confirmed Southern opinion of this intentions, and then his sudden order for relief of the fort made it clear that his policy was war. In a war, Fort Sumter would be far too important a strategic point in Southern defenses to be allowed to remain in enemy hand. It was also clear to Southern officials that if this incident did not light the fuse, another one would be arranged, and delays would only tighten the chains about the Confederacy.

How Lincoln arrived at the figure of 75,000 men to "put down the rebellion" would be interesting to know. It could not have been calculated by any competent military authority. (Before fighting ended he had put 2,213,000 men under arms). It may have been a guess based on political factors. A call for a larger number may have aroused violent opposition on the part of too many people. It is true there were only 7 states "in rebellion" at the time, but he must have known that he was forcing the other 8 to decide between Union and independence, and he must have been shrewd enough to guess the outcome. True also, he had the regular army intact except for the officers who had already resigned (enlisted men can't resign) but he knew he would lose some more when other states seceded. On the other hand, the Southern states had no army except some uncoordinated independent units, and no navy.

Each of the 8 states refused in the strongest terms to carry out his "proposed evil and unconstitutional purpose", and four of them: Arkansas, North Carolina, Tennessee and Virginia voted by tremendous margins to cast their lot with the Confederacy. Southern sympathizers in Kentucky and Missouri failed to carry their states, but they did hold separate sessions among themselves, voted for secession and sent delegates to the Confederate Congress which seated them. (They account for the 13 stars on the Confederate Battle Flag.) The Southern states that did not join the Confederacy probably sent as many men into the Confederate ranks as they did into the Union ranks.

Of the 11 states comprising the Confederacy, 4 were of the original 13: Georgia, North Carolina, South Carolina and Virginia. Tennessee came into the Union in 1796. The other six had been members less that 50 years: Louisiana 49 years, Alabama and Mississippi 42, Arkansas 25, Florida and Texas only 16. In these recent states many of the individuals who had voted to enter the Union, now disillusioned, voted to separate themselves from it. It would be unrealistic to claim that these people did this lightly or for imaginary reasons. Their way of life was being threatened and by outsiders, people who were "foreigners" to them and a threat to life itself.

The Southern states, especially South Carolina, have been criticized for seceding in the face of overwhelming odds, and Jefferson Davis has been called an "extremist", as though he induced all of them to secede. Such charges indicate an extremism of a different stripe. The record plainly shows that Davis did his best to bring about a mutual understanding between the two sections and opposed secession until, while serving in the U.S.Senate, he saw his own state secede. He sought a military post from Mississippi, not a political one. (He had graduated from West Point the year before Lee did, and had a distinguished record as a colonel in the Mexican War.) But he had presented the Southern position so well in the Senate that he had become known as "The Voice of the South", and the acclamation that greeted his election as President of the Confederate States of America thrilled the whole South: "The man and the hour have met!" Enthusiasm ran high.

Whether or not secession was the wisest course at the time
and under the circumstances depends on what the alternatives appeared to be. Southern leaders were of the opinion
that complete ruin faced the South, that the whole section
was, as George Mason had said, being bound hand and foot
and delivered into the hands of New England, that is, the
ruthless group that had become powerful through a phe-
nominal industrial development. Few Southerners were
any longer of the belief that an alternative to war could be
reached in the bitterness aroused by the abolitionists.

It is ironic that it was moderates like Davis whose efforts
had postponed secession to the disadvantage of the South.
The so-called "Fire Eaters" who had urged secession years
before were really far-sighted, radical though they were.
Had the South seceded at almost any time prior to 1860,
they would almost certainly have succeeded in gaining their
independence.

The longer the Southern states waited, the heavier the odds
against them became. The West was developing fast, and
the Northeast was rapidly gathering wealth and the technology that would produce more efficient weaponry. The interests of the border states had not swung as much toward
the North and they probably would have gone with their
sister states. On the other hand, if secession could have
been postponed just a few years, the technology of peace
might have averted it.

Such grave problems faced the 7 Confederate states that
Lincoln can almost be excused for estimating that 75,000
men could win the war in three months. Time was closing
in on the new nation. Its president was elected February 8
and its constitution adopted March 11. This was fast work,
but hundreds of administrative, diplomatic and military appointments had to be made, with the candidates for those
appointments first having to be selected and screened. Foreign nations had to be contacted and credit established, if
possible. A war time industry had to be created and some

kind of navy started, with nothing to start with in either matter. Also, fortifications had to be laid out and work begun on them.[1]

On April 13, the new government had to make its fateful decision to take Fort Sumter and a few days later face a declaration of war from the world's most powerful nation. Without support of the border states, the Confederacy lost the chance to control some strategic points.

On May 23, Virginia seceded and on July 20, the Confederate capital was moved from Montgomery to Richmond. On July 21, 30,000 northern soldiers were half way to Richmond from Washington followed by crowds of picknickers with baskets loaded with goodies for the victory celebration which must have seemed inevitable to any impartial observer.[2]

From the awful panic that followed, from the 500 dead men in blue rotting in the weeds along the banks of the sluggish Bull Run, from the thousands wounded gasping for days in the hot Virginia sun, the Northern people learned that a war was on. There were dead and wounded Southern boys too. Nobody knows how many, but despite casualties, the Southern people had the picnic that their enemy had hoped to enjoy. Not so the Southern leaders. They knew the odds, and were worried about many unanswered questions.

It had been exciting atmosphere that people were breathing in the spring of 1861 all over the country. The spirit of war was in the air. It had been building up in intensity since Lincoln's election the previous autumn. It had taken a sharp turn upward with the fall of Fort Sumter. Bands were playing martial airs in the streets of every city, and before electronic devices kept everybody's ear drums rattling, people were music hungry. A brass band thrilled its listeners from head to heel, speeded up pulses and respiration and set the feet moving in cadence. Men marching in crisp, bright uniforms with gleaming steel and fluttering flags were flanked by crowds of old and young of both sexes and colors.

War hysteria converted the two sleepy little Southern towns of Washington and Richmond into lively, crowded metropolises. Swarms of soldiers, sutlers, and office seekers strained the accomodations of both cities. All the Southern sympathizers who could do so left Washington and crossed the Potomac, heading South. All the Northern sympathizers from Richmond passed them going the other way. This population polarization took place in other areas as well.

Naturally, Negroes shared the excitement. Some pictures made in the South to spur volunteers showed a Negro boy in an ornate military hat, marching at the head of a group of recruits and beating a bass drum bigger than the boy himself. The Petersburg Daily Express of April 26, 1861 had it that 300 free Negroes about to leave the city to work on fortifications, assembled at the court house to hear a speech by ex-mayor John Dodson. Charles Tinsley, one of the free Negroes, said, "We are willing to aid Virginia's cause to the utmost extent of our ability". He stepped forward to receive the Confederate Flag, stating, "I could feel no greater pride, no more genuine gratification than to plant this flag on Fortress Monroe." Other work crews marched through the city, singing, headed for the fortifications, according to reports of the times. The Charleston Evening News said that about 125 free Negroes arrived in Petersburg, uniformed in red shirts and dark pants, all in fine spirits and carrying the flag of the Confederacy on their way to work in fortifications around Norfolk. It was a great time to be alive.

What did these Negroes know about current events and the issues involved? Probably more than might be thought. News spread rapidly in those days without the aid of modern media. Every newspaper was read and re-read many times. When people met on a road or street, they stopped and chatted, greedy for news and opinions. In the South, one always spoke to strangers and tried to draw them out, and learn about unfamiliar things. People were eager for discussion, and where two or three were gathered together, things often became lively. Others would join in for a general exchange of views and ideas. It was a time too, of florid oratory, and people hung on every word of a political speech.

Whites and Negroes were close. They heard the same speeches. They understood each other and communicated freely. One didn't have to be able to read to learn. One could listen, and ask questions, and be assured of an answer and many Negroes were constantly in attendance upon the South's most brilliant minds.

It was the habit of Southerners to talk freely in the presence of attendants and it was the habit of attendants to listen. Much gossip was passed by servants of one family to the servants of another who then passed it along to their employers. In return, gossip was brought back via the same route, and neighbors learned a great deal about each other. In the war, this was dangerous. Each side learned much about the other. Jones reports that early in the war at a top level conference in Richmond, the members adjourned for lunch and found that people in the street knew details of their confidential discussions. Throughout the war, both sides profited and both sides lost as a result of careless talk. The general who understood this danger best was Stonewall Jackson, who never mentioned his plans to anyone, not even his second in command.

What was the attitude of Southern Negroes? Were they united in purpose, and what was their purpose? Most comments in print assume that all of them were waiting with hands uplifted in piteous plea for the Yankees who had sold them into their horrible condition to come back and take them away from the customers who had bought them. It will be no news to those who have studied the facts that this is nonsense, and certainly no news to anyone that all Negroes did not think, act and look alike. They were individuals, had their own class system and their lives were affected by many influences, especially by the attitudes of people white and black around them.

Illegal slave trading had continued right up to the start of hostilities, with a peak during the decade immediately preceding, so that there were new arrivals from the African jungle working side by side with descendants of Negroes whose ancestors had been landed here 200 years before.

There is usually a big difference in attitude between "old timers" and "Johnny-come-latelies". What could have been the thoughts of these recent arrivals during the war? They had been carried off from their burning homes by armed raiders, brought to a strange land and now were seeing their new homes burned by armed raiders who wanted to carry them off again. They must have felt much in demand, but it is doubtful if it inflated their ego.

All Southern Negroes were not hoeing tobacco or picking cotton. Some were overseers, many were skill craftsmen. Many were personal servants in families where a division of sympathies existed, and would hear both sides of current political issues. Some were city dwellers, some free farmers, some (perhaps as many as 3,000 or more) were slaveholders. It is natural that their attitudes would vary, but the South was the only home that most Negroes knew, and their "white folks" were the only white people they knew and trusted. The Negro's foot was on his native hearth as was the white man's. The white people were overwhelmingly loyal to the Confederacy and it was natural that Negroes would be also.

Abolitionists and Negro slaves never seemed to get together on common ground. The abolitionist was concerned solely with "freedom" for the slave, sudden, complete, unconditional and preferably violently arrived at, if we can judge from what was said and done by the abolitionists themselves. The Negro slave was less concerned with freedom than with what his lot would be afterward. Abolitionists never worried about that, apparently.

The interlopers who came South to teach the Negroes new ways, tried to drive a wedge between them and their "white folks". From the results on record they had little success. That spring of 1861 the people of the South, white and black, slave and free, old and young, male and female, were united in their determination to make every sacrifice for the freedom of the new nation they had brought into being. They were on stage before the whole world, and the curtain was up. No people at any time ever performed more nobly in defense of their homeland, and no people have ever been more of one mind and spirit in war or peace. All had a sense of belonging to history.

Nothing human has ever been 100%, and no widespread effort or attitude has ever been unanimous, but to those of both races, representing the vast majority of each, who defended as best they could the land and the people they loved belongs the glory that courage and loyalty deserve. Especially worthy of commendation are the Negroes who were put under pressure of bribes, threats and torture by the South's enemies, and still refused to be false to their avowed loyalties.

It is hard to understand why some Negroes today would repudiate that chapter in their history for ephemeral political advantages based on unsubstantiated assumptions.

CHAPTER XVI:

EVERYBODY WORKS

The South was agricultural, and in agriculture everbody works: old, young, male, female, white, Negro, strong and weak. More than half of the slave owners had five or fewer slaves, and only 14% had more than twenty. In most families, all had to work together on the same operations for mutual survival. On the largest plantations, where the big money crops of tobacco and cotton were raised, the whites performed fewer and the Negroes more of these functions. On the small farms without slaves and on those with very few, the entire family had to put its whole weight into the problem of making a living. How many of these chores could be done with most of the white men and some of the Negroes away at war, and with many other whites and Negroes doing war work behind the lines? It was hard enough surviving with everybody staying home and working hard.

How could the soldiers be fed? If half of the food producers went into the army, how could the other half double their per-capita production? More than double it, really, because men in the army need more food than they do in civilian life. Who would weave the cloth and make the clothes for the men? Where were the mills? Who would make shoes? Marching wears out shoes at an alarming rate. How could bullets, guns, powder, swords, bayonets, and cannon be manufactured? Where were the factories and foundries? And what of horses and mules? They would be war casualties too, and how could they be replaced? It takes years for horses and mules to breed and mature, and they would need food as well as would men. But most serious, even if these problems could be solved somehow, and all these necessities produced, how could they be transported to where they would be needed by the men who would be doing the fighting? The South's railroads, already inadequate for civilian needs, would be called upon for greatly expanded service, and they would need constant repairs.

The war struck suddenly into the tranquility of Southern

life. Everybody became involved, but most of all, the plantation owners, the slaveholders, the governing class, the "indolent aristocrats" call them what you will. A wealthy planter would organize and furnish, at his own personal expense horses, uniforms, weapons and equipment for a company of cavalry and ride off at its head as captain. He might have had military experience in the Mexican War or none at all. Most were instinctively leaders, with an aptitude for matters military. A young man would pack a few belongings, usually too many, and with the blessing of his elders, order his favorite horse saddled. His lifetime Negro companion often saddled a horse for himself and refused to be left behind. From the back country, young men trudged into town with ancient weapons, sometimes even with only a pike made by lashing a Bowie knife to a hickory pole. Such was the notion of war on the part of boys who had only heard tall tales of old conflicts.

But there were men who knew what it would be like. Nearly 80,000 men had gone off only 14 years before in the war with Mexico, and only 65,000 had come back. A majority were from the South, and they still remembered what it was like to go hungry, to shiver in the cold and swelter in the heat, to be exhausted but have to keep going, and be shot at.

Most of the soldier's equipment in previous wars had come from Northern factories, but now the South would have to equip her own men with all the necessities that had formerly come from outside her borders, and not only for her armies but for her civilian population as well. Converting an efficient industrial establishment from peace time production to wartime production is a prodigious task, as this country found out in two wars during this century; but creating an entirely new industrial organization where none had existed before, and doing it while being invaded sounds impossible, but this was done in the South to an astounding degree.

Demand for industrial labor was immediate and urgent, with little or no time for training men in new skills. Whites and Negroes were taken from the sequestered rural life of the plantation and put to work in factories, foundries, shops and on fortifications, or at anything they could do to aid the war effort. What made this mad scramble so amazingly effective was the wide variety of skills that plantation workers of both races had acquired in maintaining the self-sufficient units that many large plantations were.

White men and free Negroes volunteered for war work and both were conscripted when necessary. Slaves were requisitioned from their owners and put to work where and when needed. War is not only the science of throwing lead at a distant foe; it is also the science of moving quantities of ammunition, weapons, clothing, food, fodder, and medical supplies over bad roads or no roads at all. Railroads did not run right up to the battle lines. Most war freight moved by mule, and the Negro's way with that most peculiar animal was of inestimable value.

War is also the science of moving maimed men from scenes of glory to some somewhat safer place where their arms and legs can be removed, and this also involved the Negro, the ambulance wagon and the mule. From there, the survivors of the surgery had to be removed to improvised hospitals where such recoveries as were possible depended on skillful nursing care, often, perhaps more often than not, at the hands of Negro nurses. In Richmond's Chimborazo Hospital in 1863, there were 191 white personnel of whom 166 were soldiers on guard duty; and there were 447 Negroes, of whom 264 were nurses.[1]

The South was finding the answer to many of her problems in her loyal Negroes. Their value to the South at war was commented on by General Grant, and Frederick Douglass said that slavery was a tower of strength to the South. J.H.Brewer estimates that of all the Negroes employed in Confederate war work, only about one-third were laborers.

They played their part in almost all the crafts that war requires: Wagon makers, wheelwrights, carpenters (they excelled in carpentry), coffin makers, coopers, lumbermen,

sawyers, miners, quarrymen, masons, foundrymen, blast
furnace operators, mechanics, blacksmiths, railroad engi-
neers, firemen, brakemen, repairmen, millers, painters,
shoemakers, tanners, horse handlers, cooks, barbers and
others. They were often commended for high quality work.[1]

Their numbers were never sufficient for the volume of work
to be done and those in charge of work projects constantly
complained about the shortage of help. Officials whose duty
it was to conscript labor oculd never find enough men to fill
quotas, but under Jefferson Davis, the Confederate government brought about the construction of a series of plants
throughout the South that produced a wide variety of much
needed items in great quantities.

At the start of the war, Col. T.J.Jackson (later Stonewall)
took over the armory at Harper's Ferry where he showed his
genius for war by devising a ruse that resulted in the capture of 85 B & O locomotives, most of which, by means of
man and mule power and on wooden rails, he managed to
get safely to the terminal at Winchester. Those that didn't
make it were burned, but those that did served the South
throughout the war. Jackson also removed from the arsenal
the machines for making rifles and Minie balls and sent
them to Fayetteville where they continued to turn out arms
and ammunition for the South.

The Tredegar Iron Works in Richmond was the South's
biggest plant and the only one capable of making heavy
equipment and cannon. It had manufactured railroad
trucks and cannon before the war for use throughout the nation and it had a reputation for excellence. General Joseph
Reid Anderson, the owner, was recalled from active duty in
the field to manage the works. He set up a smooth working
organization that performed miracles in production of many
much needed items, including machinery for other factories
that were being established throughout the South. He used
both free and slave Negro labor, skilled and unskilled, as
well as white labor. At its peak, the plant employed as
many as 1,200 white workers and 1,200 Negroes. (That was
equal employment.) But selections and assignments for jobs

were made strictly on the basis of which individuals could best do the particular jobs that had to be done. Tredegar was so indispensible to the Southern war effort that Richmond had to be held at all costs.[1]

The war revealed that the South was on the verge of some important industrial development, and the war was giving the development a sudden impulse. Without the war, industry undoubtedly would have developed more slowly, but the outcome of the war brought the development to an end for a long time. There had been some industry in large cities, and some Negroes had already been getting somewhat acquainted with it. Richmond's 52 tobacco factories employed 3,400 slaves and some free Negroes; but industry is not adapted to slavery, or if you prefer, slavery is not adapted to industry. Industry needs a flexible labor market, and candidates for employment with a variety of skills.[2]

The Industrial Revolution was slow in reaching the South because tobacco and cotton were so profitable, but developments were already in process to phase out the one-crop economy, mechanize agriculture and bring production of the two big crops to a point of efficiency that would make slavery uncompetitive; but the war left no chance for this to be done. Let alone, the South could have solved her own problems. The leadership was there, as the war proved, and the tragedy was that it had to be used and destroyed in a war for protection instead of being used and preserved in the peaceful improvement of a people's way of life. The only progress is growth, and growth is slow. War is not progress.

CHAPTER XVII:

HOW MANY MEN?

There were 23 states and all the federal territories lined up with the North, having a total of 22 million whites and 800,000 Negroes. There were 11 states on the side of the South with a population of 5 million whites and nearly 4 million Negroes. To a strictly impartial observer, (who would have to be from outer space) the Southern Confederacy didn't have a chance. To the world's diplomats, it must have seemed hardly worth while to put the figures down on paper; but some of them might have scratched their heads and come up with heavy support for the new nation if they had known what the South did have. It was reasonable, almost inevitable, that European diplomats would have wanted the South to win independence, not because they wished the worse for the United States but because it would be easier dealing with a division of power rather than with one large concentration of it. The South was strong, as the war proved, and Virginia was by far the strongest state of all, North and South. With two strong nations here for the rest of the world to reckon with, who knows what treaties and power balances might have been established to avoid the later eruption of two world wars? If the governments of Britain and France had known how close the South would come to achieving success, they would certainly have furnished the aid necessary to insure Confederate victory.

The disparity between North and South at the start of the war was enough to scare off the more cautious characters at home and abroad, and it soon became worse. The Southern coast, for the most part, was quickly occupied by the superior marine forces of the North, while large sections of Virginia, Tennessee, Mississippi, Arkansas, Louisiana and Texas proved to be strategically indefensible, or were fought over many times and rendered unproductive to Southern economy as well as being unproductive to Confederate conscription officers. In these areas men of Southern sympathies and of military age had volunteered early in the war and were unable to get home again to see their families until after the war's end.

Virginia's Northern Neck, which included the important city of Alexandria, had to be abandoned at the start, and the Eastern Shore counties of Accomac and Northampton were completely cut off. The mountainous western part of the state was too thinly defended and lost to the South the first year, becoming (unconstitutionally) the state of West Virginia in 1863. The second year of the war, Norfolk with its navy yard, had to be evacuated after the ironclad "Virginia" went aground and had to be burned. This key city was surrounded on three sides by deep water and exposed to bombardment from gunboats against which the South had no navy for defense.[1]

But the Commonwealth of Virginia was the heart of the Confederacy, and Richmond was the heart of Virginia. More than Richmond's psychological value, its Tredegar Iron Works made it the South's heart of steel. All the available men and munitions were concentrated in defense of the line that ran from the anchor point at Petersburg up to and including the Shenandoah Valley, Virginia's bread basket. The Army of Northern Virginia was fighting with its back to the wall, and this was the wall. Men and horses by the hundreds of thousand were marching and fighting over Virginia's northern countryside. Men were foraging for food and fodder, each man cooking his own rations, steeling fence rails and cutting down trees to make their camp fires. When people (in the North, let us hope not in the South) sing about the "watch fires of a hundred circling camps", they would do well to think for a moment of the poor farmers and their children who went cold and hungry to furnish the fuel for the fires as well as the food that was cooked on them.

Destruction was everywhere. Bridges were destroyed and rebuilt again and again, and out of wood. Fortifications and winter huts were of wood too, and the cutting of trees was done with axes and two-man saws, wielded from the fulcrum of the human sacro-iliac. The troops did their share of this work in addition to fighting, but by far the greatest amount had to be done behind the lines by field labor gangs, and these were the cut-over, fought-over areas that the South could not draw on for soldiers, work crews, factory hands or food producers. And the ruin remained long after the cannon fell silent.

The maximum percentage of a nation's total population that could be put into its fighting forces has usually been considered to be about 10%, which looks reasonable when it is realized that only 50% would be males, and of them only 50% to 60% would probably be of military age. Then, if two-thirds of these were exempted for physical disability and for civilian work essential to the war effort and to maintain the economy, the remainder for fighting duty would be about 10% of the over all total.

The total white population of the Northern states and territories, including the District of Columbia but excluding the four border states of Delaware, Kentucky, Maryland and Missouri, was approximately 19 million (18,887,500) in the 1860 census. The total white troops serving the Union from these same areas, after deducting for re-enlistments, bounty jumpers, etc., was 1,840,400, or about 9.75% of the total; but there were among them 500,000 foreign born men, one-fourth of the total force, and many were recruited abroad and not part of the 1860 census.

The total of 1,840,400 also included 86,700 substitutes hired by draftees who bought their way out of serving. (True, they had to come from somewhere, but more of that later.) The total also included 43,300 men who enlisted in the Union forces from the 11 Confederate states. If the appropriate deductions for these groups were known, it is obvious that the percentage of troops to the total population would be substantially less than 9.75%. (See Chart No.5)

Nobody without the wisdom of Solomon would venture an estimate of the total number of men in the Confederate service. Scant attention had been paid to record keeping in the Southern army because of the manpower shortages, and many of the records that were kept disappeared during and immediately after the war. Scholars have made many estimates, running from 600,000 to 1,500,000, a difference wide enough to scare off further estimating; but there are ways to narrow these extremes.

The total white population of the 11 Confederate states was approximately 5 million (5,090,200) of whom 10% would be 509,000. Deduct from this the 43,300 men who went into federal service, and add an estimate of the number of Southern sympathizers from the four border states plus West Virginia, who enlisted in the Confederate service. This estimate could be arrived at by taking 10% of the total white population of those 5 states (2,953,100) and deducting the total of Northern sympathizers who went into federal service from those 5 states (187,260). The result is 108,050 which must be added to the 509,000 after deducting the 43,300 defectors. The answer comes out 573,770, for all Confederate forces. Against the total Northern force of 2,242,960, this seems much too small.

A limit to the possible number of Confederate armed forces can be established by taking the total number of age-eligible (15 to 50) white males in the 11 Southern states (1,313,700 in 1860) and add to this the number of 13 and 14 year old lads who would be in the draft by 1864 (116,200) and deduct approximately 85,700 for the men 47 or older who would be out of the draft by 1864 when draft ages were extended. Again deducting the 43,300 defectors, produces a net total of 1,300,500 age-eligibles for the conscription officer to deal with. If he took them all, sick, crippled, and job holders essential to the war effort, he still would not have 1,500,000 as estimated by some, even after adding in the 108,050 border state men. In the North, 38% of the white age-eligibles served, but applying the same percentage to the Southern age-eligible whites brings us down to 504,700.

Estimating the size of Southern forces becomes very strange when percentages are applied to the casualties on both sides. World Almanac figures for Northern losses are 140,000 battle deaths, 224,097 other deaths, 281,881 wounds not mortal. Stanton reported 270,000 Northern men captured, putting the total losses at 916,378, or 41% of the 2,213,000 men in federal service. Confederate figures from the same source are 74,524 battle deaths, 59,297 other deaths, and 220,000 men captured (exclusive of the final surrenders.) The number of wounded is not known, but if it was twice the number of battle deaths, as the Northern figure was, then the Southern figure would be 150,000 and total Confederate losses would be 503,821. If this total of losses were 41% of the total force, then the Confederacy had 1,228,832 men under arms. Where did they come from? How could the Confederacy have raised such a large force? It would be 10% of a 12 million population, 15% of an 8 million population. And are the casualty figures correct?

Why should Northern deaths from causes other than battle (chiefly disease) be three-and-one-half times greater than Southern deaths from the same causes? Both armies occupied the same locations and were exposed to the same hazards. Germs would not discriminate between blue and gray, but if deseases attack percentages instead of actual numbers, the figure of 600,000 is again indicated. About 10% of the entire Northern force died of disease and causes other than battle, and if the same held true of Confederate forces, and the figure of 59,297 is correct then the total Confederate armed services totalled 592,970, still more than 10% of the white population even when the border state volunteers are added in. This seems much too small a force to have accomplished what the South did accomplish.

There are other factors too. The South adopted the draft early in the war, affecting white males aged 19 to 45. In 1864, a new law included ages 17 to 50, with the 17 and 18 bracket and men over 50 intended for restricted service. Also, from the start, large sections were not available for the draft and it is impossible to estimate the number of volunteers from such sections. A bewildering question is raised by foreign imports. It seems strange that the North, with such vast human resources should find it necessary to resort to recruiting men abroad. The 1860 census shows 4,100,000 foreign born in the country, mostly located in the North; but there were 500,000 men in the Northern army of foreign birth, or 90,000 more than 10% of the foreign population, indicating that 90,000 Northern soldiers, and probably more, were recruited abroad. The Confederacy also had recruiting agents in other countries, but Confederate currency didn't have the same appeal as Northern dollars, and it was harder to get any numbers through the federal blockade.

Several conclusions seem justified. The South did have a much smaller military force than the North did, probably not even half as many. Splitting the difference between the impracticably low figure of 600,000 and the impossibly high 1,250,000 would put the Confederate force at the figure of 912,500, including the border volunteers and excluding the defectors. But the Confederate population put those 43,300 men into military service, so if they are added and the border volunteers deducted, there is a figure of 847,750 representing 16-2/3 % of the 11 state population. This would be 65% of the total age-eligibles and would leave only 466,000 males including sick, crippled and those behind enemy lines to run the entire economy and all the civil affairs of the government. Was this possible?

A force of 900,000 men would have left the South outnumbered 2 1/2 to one, awesome odds indeed, especially with the North's great superiority in quality and quantity of weapons and supplies. It is hard to imagine how the South could have resisted so long with a smaller force. It should be obvious that the only reason such a large proportion of its total white population could be put into the field was because of the remarkable performance of its loyal and efficient Negro population. The North had nothing comparable, though they did have the border states. It seems evident, however, that the Negroes in the border states did not give the North the kind of service that the Southern Negroes gave the Confederacy, though claims are admittedly hard to prove; but in some sections of the border states it was mostly military occupation, not Union loyalty, that kept the populace from overtly supporting the Confederacy.

There had to be a mutual trust for white men to drop their productive work, leave farm and family to the care of their

Negroes, and defend their homes with their blood, confident that in their absence their property and loved ones would be faithfully cared for, and that if they didn't return, their families would not be abandoned. Their confidence was justified, while the war lasted. There were no strikes, no riots, revolts or outrages, even with the inevitable laxity in discipline.

CHAPTER XVIII:

TO WORK OR FIGHT

The young men who rode off or marched away from their plantation homes with the first call to arms soon became disappointed that their initial success in battle had not been pushed through to win Southern independence; and they were disillusioned by long periods of boredom in camp that followed the first engagements. Both sides were preparing for greater efforts to come.

When winter made it certain that there would be no major outbreak of fighting until spring, the more restless procured furloughs and the more reckless took French leave and went home to see how things had been going in their absence. The small farmers stayed for spring ploughing and to make sure of getting a crop in. All (or almost all) returned to the ranks in due time but not always to the same ranks they had left. Some fell in with men from other outfits who painted a more alluring picture of army life than they had been experiencing, so they casually joined with their new found friends and signed up as new recruits. This "freedom of choice" compounded the confusion that existed (and has always existed in the world's armies). As a result, men were listed as deserters in one regiment and as recruits or casualties in another. It is no wonder that Confederate military strength is so hard to estimate.

The first year of the war, General Joseph E. Johnston was in command of the armies of Virginia and General Lee was the senior member of Jefferson Davis' staff. Lee was not widely known outside of military circles, was only a colonel when he resigned from the U.S.Army, and had never commanded anything more than a regiment. As an engineer officer, he laid out the fortifications around Richmond, and was putting so many soldiers and civilians to work digging trenches that he became know as "The King of Spades". Men and boys who had rushed to the colors expecting to become heroes whacking Yankees with their swords were outraged when handed a shovel and told to join the diggers.

In the summer of 1862, the Confederate ironclad "Virginia", world's first armored battleship, went aground and had to be burned to keep her out of enemy hands, leaving the James River open to Gen. McClellan's gunboats which could have pounded Richmond to pieces in a few hours. However, every available man, black and white, alive and half alive was put to work digging gun emplacements on Drewry's Bluff a few miles down the river under Admiral Sidney Smith Lee, elder brother of Marse Robert. The gunboats came as expected but artillery fire was so heavy from the bluff that none got through to do any damage. War is the science of digging.

Thousands of slaves were home on the plantations helping the women run things. Some women proved to be capable overseers, and so did many Negroes. There were instances of loafing, irresponsibility and complaining, especially among the younger and lazier slaves, and the same kind of undertone criticism of management that one hears at the water cooler or coffee dispenser in any office or shop when the boss is away; but judging from results, at least as large a proportion of the slaves did an honest job as present day corporation employees would do with the same opportunities for shirking.

In 1907, Captain James Dinkins, ex-Confederate officer, wrote a glowing tribute to the Negroes of the South during the war, "to fulfill an obligation to a loyal and devoted people". He said he did not believe any people at any time proved themselves more loyal under the temptations that beset them, and that for months at a time many families of women and children ere wholly dependent upon their beginning of the war to the end, no incendiary language or insurrectionary movement was heard of or hinted at. Dinkins was not running for political office. He was reading a paper at the reunion of Confederate veterans in Shreveport, Louisiana.[1]

The war extended over so vast a territory that no solid line of trenches or forts could guard its entire perimeter. Efforts by one army to outflank the other were constantly being made, and foraging patrols and scouting parties were everywhere behind the lines. Northern patrols raided the homes on non-combatants, taking horses, hogs, cattle, chickens and items of personal property, even sometimes food right off the table, according to accounts related by the victims. Marauding parties often maliciously destroyed what wasn't taken. Sometimes people in the path of a raiding party drove cattle and horses into thickets and swamps until the raiders were gone, and it was a common practice to entrust silver, china and other valuables to Negroes, who buried or hid them in the slave cabins where they sometimes remained until after the war.

It is claimed that there is no record of any such treasures not being returned intact, even though raiders soon found out that the Negroes were being entrusted with valueables, and resorted to threats and even torture. It irked Northern soldiers that the Negroes who were supposed to welcome them and help destroy their white owners were actually opposing their "deliverers".

There were no Negro troops authorized by the Confederate government until almost the last few days of the war, and only one company found its way into combat. The people who always know what the coach should have done in last Sunday's game insist that the South should have armed the Negroes at the very start of the war, but there were good reasons why they didn't: (1) Negroes had never been trained for modern warfare and their adaptability to it was an unknown quantity; (2) The training would have been an immense undertaking and the pre-trained soldiery of the South had their hands full training white recruits; (3) Negroes were being used in the capacities for which they had demonstrated particular efficiency, in both skilled and unskilled work, and it was work vital to the war effort. It had to be done by somebody, and if Negroes had been put into the ranks, whites would have had to do the work. There was not only a shortage of soldiers but also a shortage of labor.[1]

General Pat Cleburne in 1864, urged the arming of the slaves, but it is hard to see how it could have been done effectively. The problem was logistics. Lee, with a line so thin that he couldn't spare men for a reserve, could not feed the men he had. Such food as there was couldn't reach the front because transportation had broken down. Still, some aver that armed slaves could have staved off the fall of Atlanta, and that peace negotiations then in progress might have ended favorably to the South. Maybe so. No one knows. Another iffy claim is that the psychological effect on Northern morale would have been devastating. Northern soldiers, seeing the people they were supposed to be liberating arrayed against them in fighting fettle, would have thrown down their arms and thrown up their hands and cried, "What in the name of the transformed Julia are we fighting for?" But soldiers don't mutiny over ideals, only over unbearable conditions when death seems a relief from a life not worth living.

The often repeated assertion that people in the South feared to trust their Negroes with arms is ridiculous. White men left home without qualms, and committed their wives and children to the care of slaves, and there were no violations of this trust. It was General Sherman who said that Negroes could not be trusted in positions of danger, but he was talking about Northern Negroes, so let them argue their own case.

Nevertheless, the experiment of training Negro soldiers was tried in the South in March 1865. In the only documented occasion of Negro soldiers as such in combat, a company from Richmond hospitals "behaved in an extraordinary suitable manner" in defending the city a couple of weeks before the break through that forced the evacuation of Richmond. Many individual Negroes did serve as soldiers and were active in combat. Some were under fire while acting in other capacities. Some were in the Confederate Navy. Many Negro "body servants" accompanied their masters to the front, foraged for them, cooked, patched their uniforms, nursed them when sick or wounded, and buried them when they died. It was not the same thing as serving in units composed entirely of Negroes where all the qualities that make up unit efficiency could be tested, but it proved the individual qualities of those who went where love and duty called.

Some Union Negro troops, captured by General Forrest on his last Tennessee raid, had been put to work on some fortifications in Mobile Bay. On an inspection tour, General Richard Taylor complimented them on their work, whereupon one of their leading members said, "Give us some guns, Marse General, and we'll fight for you too. We'd rather fight for our own white folks than for strangers". Evidently they were Southern Negroes who had been impressed into service on the Union side.

CHAPTER XIX:

CONTRABANDS

The term "contrabands" originated with General Benjamin F. Butler, U.S.A., early in the war when he was commander of occupation forces in Norfolk (and where he made himself both military commander and civil dictator, to the indignation of Edward Bates, Lincoln's Attorney General).[1] Three slaves who had been working on Confederate fortifications ran away and came within Butler's lines. The Emancipation Proclamation had not been issued, so Butler could not declare them free, but he refused to return them to their owners because (1) the Fugitive Slave Law did not apply to a "foreign country" which Virginia claimed to be, and (2) the men had worked on Confederate military installations and that made them "contraband property".[2] The theory of slavery, whether for a stated period or for life, had always been that it was the slave's services, not his body or soul, that were owned, but Butler seemed to alter this besides making the United States itself a slave owner. Academic, perhaps, but Butler was a lawyer and a Massachusetts politician, and his clever pronouncements show how a lawyer can meet himself coming and going without a nod or a word of greeting.

In November 1861, federal General Halleck ordered that no more Negroes were to be admitted within Union lines because they had been acting as Confederate spies, observing the numbers and disposition of troops and reporting back to Confederate authorities. Later this order was countermanded and other confusing orders issued, but it rather clearly indicates that there was no big rush of slaves toward the kind of freedom being peddled by the propagandists. The truth seems to be that most Negroes did not know what to think or do about freedom, and Northern officers did not know what to do about Negroes, at least the runaways and captives that came within their jurisdiction. They wanted to free the Negroes but wanted somebody else to deal with the problems involved afterward.[3]

The Negroes had no plans for after emancipation, and neither did the Northern authorities have any plans for them. Everybody was getting into something that nobody knew anything about. The Northern officers and the Negroes under their control were merely pawns of the Washington politicians who made all the decisions; but the Negroes, not unlike other people, had to eat to stay alive and, in occupied areas, it was the Northern army that controlled the source of food. Often food was obtainable only at the price of a loyalty oath. Empty bellies here, food a-plenty there. Nature abhors a vacuum, especially in the midsection.

More and more territory was coming under Northern control, and more and more was becoming a no-man's-land of battle fields, marched over and fought over by armies and raided by marauders responsible to no authority. The condition of the inhabitants, white and Negro, was hazardous. White families who could do so, gathered a few belongings and took off for some place still within Confederate jurisdiction. Some, in the belief that the invaders would not molest Negroes, left their homes and possessions in care of trusted slaves, but most of the population had to stay where they were and survive as best they could. The whites were robbed and insulted, their homes pillaged, farms ruined and their stock run off or confiscated. The Negroes were badgered and pressured to desert their white folks, and many were brought to near starvation in the process. Many unselfish and heroic deeds, unnoticed and unrecorded, were done by members of both races in attempts to help each other.

By the end of the first year of the war, New Orleans was in the hands of the North, and a great number of slaves from large Louisiana plantations were within federal lines. General Butler was transferred there and put in command. He earned the name of "Beast Butler" because of his insulting attitude toward Southern women, and the name of "Spoon Butler" because of his greed for silverware. He could have become just as unpopular without going to all that trouble. His callous neglect of the Negroes in his area could have gotten him all the disagreeable names he needed. To the question of what should be done with Negroes taken from their masters, Butler's answer seems to have been, "Nothing".[1]

General Nathaniel Banks relieved Butler in December 1862 and found that Negroes taken from their plantations were living under crowded and filthy conditions and on half rations. (They must have had some second thoughts about their "deliverers".) On January 1, right after Banks took over New Orleans, Lincoln's Emancipation Proclamation went into effect, and Banks came up with some labor rules for the Louisiana district. Planters who took the oath of allegiance were allowed to hire Negro labor at $10 per month, half of which was to be withheld until the end of the war. The workers were to receive "just treatment, healthy rations, comfortable clothing, quarters, fuel, medical attention and instruction for their children". They were not to leave the plantation without a pass, and provost marshals were to enforce "faithful service, respectful deportment, correct discipline and perfect subordination". Whipping was prohibited but loss of pay or rations would be the penalty for feigning sickness, for laziness, disobedience or insolence.

A howl went up from the abolitionists. This sounded to them like re-enslavement. Frederick Douglass and other radicals were furious. They declared that this system of labor practically enslaved the Negro and made a "mockery and a delusion" of the proclamation. Douglass said that freedom meant "...the right to choose one's own employment.....Certainly it means that if it means anything, and when any individual or combination of individuals undertakes to decide for any man when he shall work, where he shall work and for what he shall work, he or they practically reduce him to slavery. He is a slave". There was nothing the matter with Douglass when he said that. Why isn't he quoted today?[1]

CHAPTER XX:

THE PROCLAMATION

What was the real purpose of the Emancipation Proclamation? Admittedly, it was not to free all slaves, because it didn't. (It didn't even free the slaves of Mrs. Lincoln.) It was declared to be a "war measure", but in what way? How was it intended to operate toward ending the war?

Charles Francis Adams said that the prevailing belief in the North was that the proclamation would spark an immediate uprising of all the slaves in the South against their white masters and bring the war to a sudden end. The more radical abolitionists had always been hoping for more Nat Turners and more wholesale murders of white women and children. The sudden deification of John Brown in the North was especially revealing. Propagandists went about among Negroes in occupied areas, urging all of the slaves in unoccupied areas to revolt, even trying to persuade the old and crippled and the young who were too weak to carry a musket, to apply the torch to the homes of white people, their natural enemies.[1]

Lincoln, the political analyst, must have known that his proclamation would not bring on a general slave revolt, but what if it did, or didn't? He couldn't lose on this one. He was in the politically sound position that he had waited almost two years for. He had known that sooner or later he would have to take such a step to keep the support of the radical abolitionist wing, and he couldn't afford to lose that so long as the radicals retained their strength; but he also knew that if he timed the thing wrong he could lose the support of those who had been persuaded that the war was for the preservation of the Union and not for freeing the slaves.

Lincoln, the politician, knew how unstable public opinion was. The radicals packed the real power and he had committed himself to them, but he had to be prepared to jump up and run the other way if something went wrong and public opinion got out of hand. He was delaing with two forces that were not exactly congenial with each other. He was like a man courting two women, one ugly, domineering, greedy and unscrupulous, but rich; the other more comely and obliging but fickle. A man can only be true to one woman; if he tries to be true to two, he is not being true to either.

To hold the support of the sensitive people in Kentucky, Maryland, Missouri and the new state-to-be, West Virginia, Lincoln carefully avoided upsetting the slave holders in those border states, and left slavery there undisturbed. The Proclamation brought forth a wave of protests and denunciations as he knew it would, and the rate of desertions from the army increased sharply. There were anti-draft riots (we call them demonstrations now) of which the riot in New York City was one of the worst on record, resulting in the slaughter of a thousand Negroes and possibly more. A vast number of people just did not want to risk their lives for the sole purpose of freeing the slaves.

But the desertion rate levelled off, as Lincoln knew it would, and the riots were brought under control. Excesses always bring about a reaction anyway but it was timing that kept the protests from being more serious and the desertions from destroying the army. Timing was not important to the radicals. They had been clamoring for a proclamation of the kind for a long time, and always wanted it immediately. They didn't care what happened afterward. Radicals seldom if ever pause to consider what results may flow from the success of their clamorings. But timing was important to the majority of the pople, those making up what is called, for lack of a better name, "public opinion". The war news had not been good, and Lincoln, with his Proclamation all prepared, was waiting for the proper moment. The moment came on September 22, 1862, following Lee's withdrawal from Maryland after the Battle of Sharpsburg (Antietam).

If the radical abolitionists had hoped for mass murders in proportion to what happened in the French West Indies, They had to be satisfied with zero. The Negroes in the Southern states went about their daily activities with no intention of murdering anybody, and there was no visible reaction among them to the proclamation. Actually, the only thing the proclamation accomplished was pacification of the abolitionists. They wanted it, and Lincoln gave it to them. It is a rule of politicians to give a bloc of organized voters anything they demand regardless of costs (to other people) unless their demands are opposed by another bloc with more voters. The opponents of the proclamation were not organized.

Lincoln's Emancipation Proclamation was anticipated nearly 100 years before by Lord Dunmore's emancipation proclamation of 1775 in Norfolk, Virginia, but Dunmore's timing was wrong and he reversed Lincoln's series of moves. This unpopular Royal Governor of Virginia first seized arms and powder in Norfolk on the pretext that he feared a slave uprising. Shortly thereafter he armed several hundred Negroes that he had "freed". Then he issued his general proclamation, as a war measure. But he lost the war.

CHAPTER XXI:

OVERDRAFTS

Authorization was issued for the recruitment of Negro troops to fight against the South, and a great rush of volunteers was expected. Northern people thought, "NOW the Southern slaves will come swarming into our lines begging for muskets!" But the rush never got going. Recruiting officers and state "agents" did their best but couldn't meet quotas. Economic conditions in the South were bad and getting worse, and most of the Negroes who did come voluntarily into the Union lines were just hungry. They were willing to work for something to eat but didn't want to fight against their own people. Enormous pressure was put on them. They were bribed, coaxed, ridiculed, browbeaten, and if they still wouldn't hold up the right hand they were given arduous and disagreeable tasks to perform until they broke down and agreed to "volunteer". Negroes living in enemy occupied territory were similarly treated, and when the draft was extended to include Negroes, they were also included. Many Negroes then fled into the woods and swamps to avoid being drafted, and patrols hunted them down like criminals. Some were even shot, it was charged.[1]

There were thousands of destitute Negroes living in this half-world of Yankee occupied Rebel territory. They were a great pool of recruits for Lincoln's forces; and perhaps they can explain what is wrong with Chart No.4.

When a man's number came up in the draft, he had the choice of shouldering a musket or buying his way out by paying somebody hungry enough or thirsty enough, or perhaps just fascinated by the look and smell and feel of money to sign up in his stead. There were 86,724 men who bought out, so there had to be plenty of substitutes available, although there were "repeaters" or "bounty jumpers", men who signed up, got paid, deserted and signed up again. In buying a substitute, a draftee might get one of these slightly used "heroes born of woman" to perform his patriotic duty for him; but the fact that his rightful place in the "burnished rows of steel" would be a little tarnished didn't embarrass the draftee because the transaction was handled by brokers and the draftee would see none of the sordid details.

The total of 86,724 purchase-and-sale transactions was big business, requiring the services of trained and efficient middle men. A draftee only needed to make the proper contact, or perhaps a broker would make contact with him when his number came up, but either way, everything would be smoothly handled from there on. Destitute Southern Negroes within Union lines could be hired for little more than a good meal, but brokers would charge their draftee clients the full going price. This practice was carried to the extreme, as most practices always are, and it became so notorious that orders went out that white draftees could hire only white substitutes (and presumably Negro draftees could only hire Negroes). Before the end of the war, the practice of hiring substitutes was abolished.

This explains the discrepancies in Chart No.4. A substitute would ordinarily be credited to the draftee's own state, but hiring Negroes fouled up the statistics. The percentage of the total Negro population serving in the armed forces runs from 3% in Massachusetts to 330% in Kansas, with some of the other state statistics just as unrealistic. You can't have more Negro soldiers than there are Negroes. (It is only fair to mention that the South had the draft before the North did and the substitute system as well. There were abuses in the South too.)

As the devastation of war spread over more and more of the South, more and more Negroes yielded to pressure and joined the Union forces. Some had seen their white folks killed or scattered, their homes burned, stock run off and the once fertile fields grown up to weeds and brush. What was there to return to? Not that they wanted to return to slavery, but the only home they knew was gone, and what they were experiencing was not what they thought freedom would be like. But who knows what they thought freedom would be like? The majority, that is. Perhaps they thought it would be like their old way of life with a lot of improvements, but it seems unlikely that any number of them who joined the Union ranks did so because they thought that would help them attain it. By this time, in any event, most of them had seen enough to have some doubts about freedom U.S.Army brand. One would think so, at least. Those who had been in sympathy with the North at the start had been among the first runaways, and first in the ranks of the new Negro army units. How many there were it is impossible to say because all recruits undergo psychological changes during both training and service.

Negro troops were not actually needed in the Northern army. The Northern population had not furnished its full potential of military recruits, and there were many men who could have been drafted as replacements for existing units. The training problem of Negroes whose lifetime habits had not fitted them well for army life was difficult and took time. The necessity for doing something with the Negroes who had accumulated within the Union lines was partly a practical problem. Did it occur to anyone to re-locate these Negroes in Northern communities and employ them in Northern mills and offices? However, the problem was also political. The abolitionist attitude required justification and so did the Emancipation Proclamation. Army officers were pressured into organizing the Negroes and seeing that they made a good record.

Lincoln was extremely sensitive where politics were concerned. Fraud and other forms of corruption were everywhere but he would do nothing about them if there were no political involvements. The diary of Edward Bates, Attorney General, contains many references to Lincoln's weakness in dealing with those who had political power. He would not give Butler a well deserved call-down for making himself a petty tyrant in Norfolk because Butler might stir up a "hubbub"; and Bates was disgusted because Lincoln would neither control Stanton (Secretary of War) or get rid of him. "He knows the problem", said Bates, "But lacks the nerve to apply the remedy".

When one of his political dykes sprang a leak Lincoln was quick to shove a finger into the hole; and when, for instance, complaints reached him that Negroes under some of his generals were being mistreated, he wrote directly to the generals demanding that the practices be stopped.[1] He even insisted that a direct reply be returned to him. He did not just refer the matter to Stanton and let it go at that. The abolitionist radicals were sensitive about maintaining the popular belief that only "indolent" Southern aristocrats mistreated Negroes. But there were no politics involved when more than once complaints reached Lincoln directly that Confederate prisoners of war were mistreated, issued food unfit to eat and in quantities scarcely sufficient to sustain life, given inadequate clothing and blankets for winter weather. Lincoln merely turned these over to Stanton who, he knew, was deliberately responsible for the complained of conditions and would either ignore the whole thing or wreak a contemptible revenge by increasing the mistreatment and reducing the meagre fare handed out. At Fort Douglas, 10% of the Confederate POW's died in one month.[2]

The Adjutant General's office has the figure of 186,017 as the total number of Negro troops recruited during the war. J.T.Wilson estimates that there were 220,000. The World Almanac gives 200,000, and Official Records (p.237) says 178,985 including 7,122 officers who were white, leaving a net total of Negroes under arms of 171,863. This last estimate seems more in line with the total Negro population from which the soldiers were drawn. However, Official Records states that 37,300 Negroes lost their lives in the service, which seems extraordinarily large in proportion not only to the total force but to the limited number of engagements and field duty in which Negroes participated. Actual battle losses reported are small in comparison with total deaths. The Negroes came in late and most of them were used for garrisoning forts, doing general guard duty including, unfortunately, guarding prisoners of war.

Wiley lists three battles that constituted most of the combat duty for Negroes: Port Hudson, Milliken's Bend, and the Petersburg Crater. Their total losses for all three battles were 347 killed, 1,137 wounded and 801 missing, and some of these were white officers. The figure of 37,300 needs some study and explaining. It is 21% of all Negro troops enlisted whereas total deaths among white troops amounted to 16%.

The truth about the performance of Negro troops during that war may never be known. The official reports of the officers are open to the suspicion of false claims of great accomplishments because of the sensitive political situation in which the officers found themselves. They had to turn in favorable reports no matter what happened. Officers had been dismissed from the service for objecting to assignments with Negro units. Any criticism or even lack of praise might bring a storm of charges of bias, prejudice, and all the smear terms that are still good today for political purposes. Complaints were bound to reach Lincoln himself, and ambitious officers might have to look outside the service for some other fulfillment of their ambitions. Extravagant assertions about the behavior of Negro troops under fire and about their total contribution to the war effort could have been the truth or they could have been put into the record simply because they would come to Lincoln's attention and aid his delicate relationship with the radicals.[1]

Official Records are full of reports by Northern officers that are vague, bombastic and boastful. One in particular is General Pleasanton's extravagant report of the Battle of Brandy Station. Among other things he stated that General Lee's plans had been captured. He didn't say he had seen them, or that they had been reported to him as captured. He made it a flat statement. It was entirely untrue and was proven so shortly afterward, but it was reported in later accounts of the battle and is still to be seen in current accounts. But compare Pleasanton's report with the simple, factual report of his opponent, General J.E.B.Stuart. one reason for the great difference between reports of federal officers and those of Confederates is that the reports of Northern officers were used for political purposes by political generals.

It is said that Lincoln was once asked if he knew how many men the South had under arms. "Precisely", he said, "Ten million. We have one million and all my generals assure me that they are outnumbered ten to one". There was less need and less time for such politicking in Southern armies, and besides, the reports of Southern officers went to generals like Lee, Jackson, Forrest, Longstreet and some others who would not be deceived by puffing.

The worst result of these overblown battle reports was that those Negroes whose behavior was praiseworthy have been robbed of any genuine assurance that the commendatory cliches lavished upon them will be believed. On the other hand, the accounts of meritorious performance on the part of Southern Negroes leave little doubt that the praise given was deserved because there was no political advantage to be gained by exaggeration or flattery.

Northern Negroes were no "tower of strength" to the North as Southern Negroes were to the South. They represented only about 1 -1/4% of the total population except for the border states and there loyalty was divided, and the facts are hard to arrive at. With plenty of manpower in the North, the labor performed by Negroes was not indispensible. Their presence was, in fact, a negative influence on morale as shown by the savage draft riots and the wave of desertions that followed Lincoln's proclamation. As the North acquired more Negroes from the Southern areas, problems increased. Training of Negro units, undertaken midway in the war, was limited in what it could accomplish. Through no fault of the Negroes, their participation had little if any effect on the outcome of the war.

CHAPTER XXII:

PSYCHOLOGICAL WARFARE

If the war had really been for preservation of the Union, many things that did happen during and after the actual fighting could never have happened. There were unlimited opportunities for building up good will between the people of the two sections during the war itself, more especially during the fighting, perhaps, because the people of the North and the people of the South, who had lived apart from each other, were now face to face in large numbers. They were fighting, it is true, but enemies can respect each other, and often the men in the ranks were glad to fraternize. But it was when large forces accupied Southern territory and came into contact with the wives and children of Confederate fighting men that the greatest opportunity existed for cementing the two sections together.

Simply by showing non-combatants common courtesy and respect for their persons and property, a humane leadership would have accomplished much if that had been the policy of those at the head of the federal government. There were instances when civilians were treated with consideration, but they were only incidences, the voluntary acts of Northern officers and men who happened to have good breeding and self respect. They were not the result of Northern political policy or military strategy. On the contrary, these acts of kindness seemed to be violations of a policy designed to establish relations of the very worst sort. Citizens of the South were regarded as having no rights at all, and from the very first the vandalism and pillage often appeared to be at the direction of the general officers or at least with their tacit permission. Some units were more notorious than others, and among the worst were the ones recruited abroad consisting of mercenaries.

No real attempt was made by Northern policy directors to understand and ameliorate the problems that their presence created. It was as if they were in some foreign land for the purpose of destroying it wholly, as the Romans destroyed Carthage, its rival, by ploughing up its cities and sowing the land to salt. In the last year of the war, total destruction did become the avowed official policy agreed upon by Lincoln, Stanton and Grant. They watched with satisfaction as one-fourth of what they called their own country was being reduced to ruins and ashes by Sherman, Sheridan and Hunter, enjoying the joke attributed to Grant but more characteristic of Lincoln's humor, that a crow flying over the Shenandoah Valley would have to carry its own rations with it. Perhaps Edgar Allen Poe, who died a dozen years before the war, had a prophetic vision when he wrote about "the greenest of our valleys" being assailed by "evil things in robes of sorrow".

A disinterested observer, if there had been one, would have been justified in concluding that the purpose of the North was to exterminate the Southern whites, confiscate their land and re-enslave their Negroes. In fact, this purpose was expressed almost in so many words by the architects of Reconstruction.

Northern politicians and propagandists had more success in driving a wedge between the whites of the two sections than they did in driving a wedge between the Southern whites and their Negroes (during the war, that is). Northern people thought they understood the attitude of both Southern whites and Negroes. They believed that each had only one thought in mind: The Negro, freedom, the white, slavery. It bewildered them that all the Negroes did not run away when they were given the chance, but they were sure the Negroes were beaten and brutalized by the whites and that the white were "prejudiced" and therefore hated all Negroes.

The Northern definition of "prejudice" is hard to express. The word actually means arriving at a judgement before giving reasonable consideration to evidence. Northerners who had never known a Negro personally were well aware that Southerners had known many Negroes and lived in close association with them all their lives, but were sure that the whites were "prejudiced". Perhaps they reasoned that Southerners ignored the evidence, otherwise Southerners would have the same ideas and notions as Northerners; and it was with this comfortable assurance that they understood everything about racial relationships that the invaders arrived. They expected to find long lines of slaves with outstretched hands begging to have their manacles struck off. They never quite understood why the long lines didn't show up, but they clung to their ideas just the same.

These avowedly unprejudiced observers saw slavery for the first time, and many were seeing Negroes for the first time, but they wrote home to the folks who were eagerly waiting for news and told them that slavery was everything they had always belived it was. How could they do otherwise? Who would risk being branded traitor to the cause, or under the spell of the languid habits of indolent slaveowners or, worse, captivated by some bewitching Southern belle?

The invaders did not know that they couldn't see Southern life as it really was, for one thing, their very presence had changed it. Life there had changed even before the invaders arrived. The Northern stranger didn't know, and upon advice of politicians would not believe that relationship between Southern whites and Southern Negroes was normally an easy going thing without strain, mutually considerate, each recognizing a duty to the other that most of them performed to the best of their ability.

Before war came, life in the South was bright, a thing to be enjoyed and passed along to succeding generations as a blessing. People were gracious, courtesy was spontaneous. There was an indescribable spirit that could be felt but not expressed. How could an invader whose job it was to kill and destroy be expected to sense such a spirit and such a relationship especially when he was determined to find just the opposite?

Northern officers never stopped to think that Southern Negroes did not enjoy seeing their white folks killed and their

homes burned. They didn't understand that to Southern
Negroes the Southern white people were their own people,
the homes and farms their own too, and that however unin-
structed the Negroes might have been on the issues involved, and however much Northern propaganda they may
have heard, they would still be suspicious of strangers coming with force of arms to destroy the peace that they all had
enjoyed. If the officers had asked themselves what they
themselves would have thought of outsiders coming into
their own towns with promises of a better life but commit-
ting acts of violence and wanton destruction, they might
have altered their techniques.

Federal officers interviewed many Negroes, mostly to their
own bewilderment. Some confessed that they were amazed
at the shrewdness with which the Negroes could tell what
answers were expected of them and never fail to give their
inquisitors what they wanted to hear. Some of their answers are still taken seriously and appear in present day
publications. The Negroes well knew the futility of giving
answers that would be unfavorable to the new order of
things. They knew that they would be unable to change
what was happening. They were under new masters and
would have to adapt themselves. They greeted the newcomers with customary courtesy, listened to what was told them
and carried out instructions; but the strangers knew that
the Negroes were not giving them the same respect that
their Southern white folks received, though they never
knew why. The reason was that the Northern strangers
were not giving the Negroes the same thing in return.[1]

The recruitment of Southern Negroes to fight against Southern whites was not a war necessity. Aside from political reasons, it was done in a spirit of vengeance, certainly not in a
spirit of preserving the Union or cementing the two sections
of the country together. Apparently no one in the North
ever stopped to think that if the North won, the two sections
would be part of the same country again, and all people
would have to live together in friendship. Seeing their own
Negroes arrayed in blue uniforms enraged the white people

of the South, though their anger was directed at Northern leaders, not so much at the Negroes. The pressure exerted to gain recruits was well understood, as was the fact that all soldiers have to obey commands. It was, however, unfortunate that Stanton was permitted to use Negro troops for guarding prisoners of war, and carry out his brutal, vengeful policy through them. The best combat troops are usually not assigned to guard duty anyway, and from all accounts of POW treatment, Stanton must have selected his guards from among the worst. Too many instances have been reported and too much evidence brought to light to leave room for doubt that brutal treatment of Southern prisoners was deliberate official policy. No one knows how much Stanton damaged the Negro image.[1]

Lincoln, as commander in chief, made it his business to know everything that was going on. He well knew how vicious Stanton was and how he treated prisoners as well as non-combatants in occupied areas, but there was no political advantage to be gained by putting a stop to his practices. On the contrary, it might have cost him support from the industrial power pack that supported the abolitionists. Suppose Stanton created a hubbub and went to the people with the charge that Lincoln was "soft" on secessionists? But of course Stanton could not have been solely responsible. There seems no reason to think that Lincoln himself felt any differently. Having Stanton do the dirty work enabled him to wash his hands as Pilate did.

Stanton's 1866 release shows 270,000 Yankees in Rebel prisons with 22,576 deaths (8.3%) against 220,000 Rebels in Yankee prisons with 25,436 deaths (12%) a death rate almost 50% greater.

CHAPTER XXIII:

END AND BEGINNING

As the war drew near its end, the invading armies were burning more homes and barns and crops, destroying more bridges, railroads, canal locks, and occupying more territory. The amount of land for food production was shrinking, and so was the number of people to work the land. Horses and mules, wagons and railroads were too few and too poor to carry the food to the people in the cities or even to the starving armies. Material for repairing anything could not be found, nor could skilled hands to do the work. Locomotives and cars came to a dead halt for want of parts. Replacements for horse and mule casualties in the army were taken from the transportation of food. Clothes and uniforms faded, wore out, were tattered and went threadbare, but patches were worn proudly "for the Cause" and individuals well dressed or well fed were looked upon with suspicion.

Materials vital to everyday living were not to be had in most places at most times. Cooking utensils wore out and couldn't be replaced. Salt had been scarce for three years, and there is no substitute for salt. Without it, hams and bacon could not be cured. Sugar and coffee were impossible to get. Parched corn, wheat or roasted sweet potato shins made something that looked like coffee and could usually be kept down when swallowed especially if sweetened with sorghum molasses. Milk was hardly available at all. It had to be used where produced because there was no refrigeration and no way of transporting it anyway. Cows were confiscated by the enemy or slaughtered by starving people, and babies went without milk. Sasafrass and blackberry leaves made a kind of tea. Cooking soda was made from the ashes of corn cobs. Pine knots served as candles, and grease with woolen rags for wicks were used for lamps. The invading armies lived off the land, using up all the cattle, hogs, chickens, feed and hay they could find.

The same privations were borne by all civilians, white and

Negro, and by all soldiers and officers, even the generals, and, necessarily, prisoners or war. Southern authorities were accused of reducing rations for POW's to a bare subsistence level, and many people in the North still believe the charges that are still kept alive. Many do not even know today how very little and uncertain the Confederate soldier's rations were. The truth is that prisoners of war were given more and better food than Confederate soldiers, for the obvious reason that the soldier could supplement his meagre portions by foraging, while the POW could not. If the Confederacy had issued the same food to prisoners as to their own troops, as the rules of war required, the prisoners would have starved to death.

The difference between Northern plenty and Southern starvation fare was gruesomely illustrated on the battlefield. One could tell at a glance which dead were Yankees and which Rebels. The corpses that had swollen to enormous size were the well fed Yankees; those that were gaunt and drawn were Rebels who had been just as cadaverous looking before death struck.[1]

Among the many shortages of vital materials were medicines and medical instruments, hampering treatment of prisoners as well as soldiers and civilians. It was getting harder to run the blockade, and many drugs could no longer be smuggled in. The North discontinued exchanging prisoners, and refused offers from the Confederate government to allow Northern surgeons to enter POW camps and treat their own men, or to admit supplies for prisoners only. During this time there were many more Northern men in Southern prisons than Southern men in Northern prisons, but the Confederate government offered to exchange all the men they held for all the men held in the North. Even though this uneven exchange would be numerically very much to Northern advantage, Grant telegraphed Lincoln that it "would insure Sherman's defeat" and the offer was refused. But why would it "insure" Sherman's defeat? It is worth pondering what Grant had in mind.[1]

It took Grant almost a year to breach the thin line that stretched from Richmond to Petersburg, though he had vastly more men, better arms, heavier guns, plenty of ammunition, food, medical supplies, efficient transportation, and an unlimited reserve upon which to draw. Lee had no reserves to throw in when a concentrated attack was made. His men had to stand and hurl the enemy back, but always some died and made the line thinner. Then the line got too thin to hold, the South had run out of men and all the things that men need for war. After all the "ifs" have been disposed of, the "why-didn't-they's" and the "should-have's", it all reduces to arithmetic. Lee had swapped one of his for two of theirs, but with a limited supply against an unlimited supply, there could be only one result.

The South, after four years of war, the rich South, was more dead than alive, a nation exhausted by superhuman effort against overwhelming numbers and quantities. The men who left the Richmond-Petersburg trenches and fell back toward Appomattox were exhausted and hungry, and short of ammunition. Lee had needed more men, but there was no food and no supplies for the men he had. There was food elsewhere but no way to get it to the front. The South had run out of everything. The effort was total. When the sun went down upon the Confederacy, the stars shone on the faces, white and black, of those who had done all that could be done in defence of their homeland. The glory and the suffering were shared by all, to all belonged the consciousness of duty faithfully performed.

There are fourteen graves at Appomattox, in which lie the men who paid full price for the last day's performance. Perhaps they were the lucky ones. They died soldiers and citizens of their beloved and still alive Confederacy and did not have to witness its extinction. The other ragged paupers staggered into line, numb to the strange world around them, struggling to rid their minds of the cloudy notion that Marse Robert was surrendering. Somebody had at last found a reasonably   white shirt to display and the firing had stopped. Stragglers were still limping up, but everything was so quiet. Word was passed around, "Officers, keep your side arms. Officers and men keep your horses, those who have them. Give your parole, go to your homes and remain there until exchanged". Some color bearers took their tattered Battle Flags off their staffs and stuffed them under their tattered shirts.

Then the last of the Great Gray Army melted like mist, diffusing itself into small groups that became smaller at each cross roads until each man turned away from his comrades on a lonely last leg of the journey home. It was a long walk for some, hundreds of miles. They must have done a lot of thinking as they trudged along, stopping at wayside houses to beg a bit of corn pone and exchange news, and sleeping wherever they could find shelter from the chill of April nights. As they passed deserted and ruined farms the future must have looked bleak. They must have wondered how long they could hold on to their own farms, how they could put in a crop with no money, no stock and, for the larger operators, no slaves. Some wondered how it would be possible to tolerate the domination of the forces that had destroyed their way of life, and plans for migration to foreign countries did take shape in some minds, and some were later carried out.

Most, however, felt that there was a basis for hope, and that recovery would be encouraged and not obstructed by the new regime. Possibly life would not be so very different. Everybody was in the same boat. They would get together with their neighbors and talk things over. Something could be worked out.

Up North, things were different. The telegraph, that marvel of the age, clicked out the surrender news all over the North and West at the same instant, and every man, woman and child simultaneously drew in a deep breath and gave forth with a mighty cheer. People ran about with faces radiating excitement, telling each other the great news that the long war was over at last. Everybody already knew it but everybody wanted to hear it again. The local orators sud-

denly had an eager audience and a subject that couldn't
miss getting the wild cheers and thunderous applause that
orators live only for. Men jeopardized their own health
drinking the health of Lincoln, Grant and their home town
heroes; and the people who didn't drink seemed just as
drunk as those who did. A powerful wave of euphoria had
engulfed the whole country lying beyond the borders of the
Confederacy.

Stanton telegraphed orders to every fort and arsenal all
over the nation that a salute of 200 guns be fired, and every
gun in the country belched long tongues of fire, huge billows
of thick gray smoke and deep reverberations of noise. The
wonderful telegraph could have synchronized the measured
booming of the cannon so that every square foot of earth
from Maine to California would vibrate at the same moment
in 200 intervals; but the Secretary of War was so anxious to
have his victory proclaimed to the world that he failed to
think of this ultimate refinement.

When the last great "BOOM!" had shaken the ground, and
the last great billow of drifting gray smoke had evaporated
as the great gray Army of Northern Virginia had evaporated, there was a muffled "pop" from a small hand gun in
Washington.

With emotions at the height of intensity, the thin veil between laughter and tears was torn asunder; but at first
there were no tears. Cheering came to a sudden bewildered
halt as people everywhere looked at each other in silent un-
belief. Some people even stopped drinking. The public
mind, The Northern public mind, was shocked into momen-
tary paralysis. The collective cerebrum was blank. Then it
was announced that the assassin was a Southern sympa-
thizer. That wrote in big black letters on the country's big
blank thinking space the verdict "GUILTY" against every
white person in the South; guilty of assassination, the vilest
form of murder, and of a President, the vilest form of assassination, and of Lincoln, the most perfect of presidents. The
vipers of vituperation revived and poured out upon the col-

lective head of Southerners,- white Southerners, the most virulent venom ever.

CHAPTER XXIV:

A WAR BY ANY OTHER NAME

With the murder of Lincoln, masks started coming off and light started shining into dark corners, but the public refused to look, for to do so might destroy too many cherished notions. Destroying a pet notion is like shooting a faithful dog.

Up to the end of the war, it was easy for the Northern public to believe the official propaganda, though they didn't call it propaganda then. That term came in with World War I. But from the behavior of Congress, particularly congressional leadership, busy creating the chaos called "reconstruction", how could the public believe any longer that this had been a war for the preservation of the Union? Lincoln gave it the name of "The War of the Rebellion", a necessary term if the Southern leaders were to be smeared as "traitors"; but he knew that the war was not just an effort on the part of a group of Southern individuals to rebel against constitutional authority and overthrow the government. Lincoln even charged in his Gettysburg address that it was an effort to destroy the whole concept of government by the people, for the people and of the people. On the other hand, there was an unconstitutional usurpation of authority on the part of Northern states and of Lincoln himself which could more properly be called rebellion. It was the seceding states that really acted according to constituted authority, that is, authority in accordance with the constitution. (Oddly, however, while Southerners resent the war being called "The War of the Rebellion", they cherish the name "Rebel" and delight in being called "Rebels". Originally intended as a slur, it was embraced lovingly by Southerners and made a name to conjure with.)

Up to now, no satisfactory name has been seriously suggested for that war. "The American Civil War", the commonly accepted name, does not seem appropriate. It designates the war as a companion piece to the English Civil War of 200 years previously and is in no way related to it. The English Civil War was between two groups within the same geographical boundaries, both struggling for control of the same government, each group different in political philosophy. Here the war was a struggle between two separate nations, the same as in most wars, for the South was in fact a separate nation and was not struggling for control over the North, only defending itself against aggression.

Chief opposition to the name "American Civil War" has come from the war's greatest historian, Dr. Douglas Southall Freeman who insisted on the "War Between the States", and it certainly was that, but the name does not say what states or why a war. "The War for Southern Security", another suggestion, sounds like a war plotted for acquisition of territorial buffers, as in Europe. Even more obscure is the suggestion "The Last Capitalist Revolution", whatever that was supposed to mean. Did the Capitalist North revolt against the Constitution? It did, of course, but was it the last?

Stonewall Jackson's preference was "Our Second War of Independence" and others have proposed "The Second American Revolution" and "The War for Southern Independence". All of these identify it with the war of 1776. Both were for independence, also for freedom from arbitrary political domination and economic strangulation; but there were important differences. The American Revolution was really a rebellion, a defiance, a breaking of the faith. The people of America had sworn loyalty to the king, and were then throwing off that loyalty and deposing the king in America, whereas the people of the South had sworn loyalty to the Constitution, NOT the Union, and were keeping their faith with the Constitution. They took the Constitution with them essentially intact and adopted it as the Constitution of the Confederacy. The South was not fighting to establish a new order, but only to reclaim old rights that had been taken away.

They justified their action on principles clearly stated in the Declaration of Independence, and Virginia was exercising an option that was a condition of her ratification of the Constitution itself.

Until a couple of years prior to 1776, many Americans wanted to fight for their rights as Englishmen under the king, and later on, during the war the king offered to grant all demands except independence. However, a negotiated settlement of the main issue, taxation without representation, might have left the colonies with minority representation to be always outvoted by the majority that was exploiting them; and Americans would have been in the same intolerable position as the South found itself in 1860.

For stark truth, the so-called "Civil War" ought to be called "The War For Destruction of the South". It was as much a war for destruction as any war that was ever fought on this or on any continent. It is surprising, nevertheless, how often the question is asked, "What was the South fighting for anyway?" and the usual answers are just as surprisingly vague and involved. The real answer is quite simple. The South was fighting because it was invaded.

A remark just as often heard, even in the South is, "Well, it all turned out for the best". But did it? And best for whom? The ones who were killed? For those who lost husbands, sweethearts, children? For the thousands of Southern people who lost homes and fortunes and a long established peaceful way of life? For the next two or three generations brought up in poverty created by the war's destruction? Or for America, the country, that lost the source of much brilliant leadership, and the lives and services of many fine people? And didn't the war destroy our form of government and substitute another? A government of limited and different powers was replaced by a government of consolidated powers. That war started big government on its way to becoming too big.

Then one hears, "But aren't we better off now?" which has a built-in answer, "Of course we are", which implies that a nation can better itself by killing off many of its finest lives and destroying much of its most valuable property. If fighting each other improved our nation so much, why don't we do it more often?

But it is interesting to speculate upon who are meant by "WE" when it is said that "we" are better off. Presumably "we" means the present inhabitants of this land; but who knows how well off the inhabitants of this land would be now if there had been no war? Certainly WE would not be the present inhabitants of this or any other land. WE would be still in the limbo of unborn souls, if there is such a thing, had the war not disrupted the forces of selection that determine who shall and who shall not be born. Each germ of life is a potential individual, and out of the billions of eligible candidates for life in human form, WE were selected. Never mind why, but HOW? By an obviously complex process influenced by millions of conditions and events; and the odds against any one particular individual being born are in the range of billions times billions or even greater. The odds can be vastly altered by the most obscure factors and the war was certainly not obscure. Without the war, entirely different individuals would now be living here. Because of the war, WE occupy the place of others who had a right to be born in our stead.[1]

CHAPTER XXV:

LEGALISMS

To the Confederate soldier on his way home from the war, news of the assassination was disturbing. Without any love for Lincoln, he asked himself why it was done now that the fighting had ended, and he wondered how the upset in government would alter matters for the South. The Vice President, Andrew Johnson, was a Southerner, a Tennessean, but an enemy of the Confederacy. Native born enemies were despised. Yankees might be hated collectively, but individuals could be respected; not so those Southerners who calculated the odds and turned against their own people because prospects looked brighter for them that way. There would never be forgiveness for any "tallow faced buffalo".

Johnson's motivation, however, seemed to have been resentment. He was from the poorest of the poor whites, his education being only what he got from his wife, a teacher. He was a tailor and always made his own clothes, even in the White House. He got himself elected to public office originally by haranguing the most miserable of his constituents about how he had advanced himself despite his own lack of advantages and how he would help them to a better life. It was an ancient line then but effective and still seems to be so. But Johnson drank too much at times, even when president; and on the most inappropriate occasions he would get off on the subject of his early poverty and lack of education.

Johnson hated and resented members of the slave holding class, not because they owned slaves but because they had cultural advantages he did not. He carried a monstrous inferiority complex all the way to the grave.

He not only despised slave owners, he also despised Negroes and did not want either to participate in government. The only reason he wanted slavery ended was that the slaveowners would be injured thereby. He was not in any sense an abolitionist. Southerners believed that his ascendancy to the presidency would change everything for the worse. They were wrong because they did not know why Lincoln was murdered. They taught their children and their children's children that if Lincoln had lived, the horrors of Reconstruction would not have occurred. They were wrong again because they did not know the real reason for Reconstruction.

To the soldier, the war was over. He had fought for Southern independence and had failed to win it. He would have to respect the decision of war. How to pay taxes, rebuild, get money to buy stock and equipment, these were the problems that occupied his mind. The political problems he thought would be simple, with perhaps some complications because of the assassination; but he assumed that his state was now back in the Union inasmuch as the Union forces had accomplished their declared intention to get it back and Lincoln had insisted that it had never been out of the Union. Why there should be any complications he could not see, which is not strange because few have understood why since, judging by the diversity of opinions even today and the acceptance of illogical conclusions.

The position taken by Lincoln when the states first seceded was unsound, unconstitutional and dishonest, adopted solely because it was the only position that furnished the federal government an excuse for sending military forces into the South. The legalism that he dreamed up presumed that the Union existed before the states and was indestructible, that a state could not secede and that the Union was therefore unbroken. This ignored the fact that some states, notably Virginia, had ratified the Constitution with the expressed proviso that they could repeal ratification if things worked out to their disadvantage. His change of rules in the middle of the game held that the individuals responsible for the attempted secession had rebelled against federal authority. This ignored another fact: that secession had been voted by an overwhelming majority of the people and/or their legally elected representatives, and that even those people who voted against secession accepted the course their states had taken, and put their lives on the line. Lincoln could not but be well aware of the true facts. If a state is not its people and their duly elected representatives, what is it? Lincoln's position indicted the entire white population of the South (and almost all of the Negro population too) and convicted them of treason without a trial. Did he intend to hang everybody in the South?

If the federal government had recognized the constitutional right of a state to secede, any attempt to coerce the Southern states back into the Union would have been aggression, but it would have permitted Lincoln and Davis to meet as equals, politically, and negotiate for peace. Even without conceding the right of a state to secede, Lincoln could have met with Davis, even unofficially and off the record. Davis wanted union, and if Lincoln had wanted union and no other political advantage he would not have been afraid to trust peaceful negotiation. His pseudo-legal concept immediately cut off all possibility of peace. His position was designed to cover up the aggressive purpose of the Northern industrial war party, and it did it well (so well that it still deceives people) but with the war over, its usefulness was at an end. One fundamental fallacy had to give way to another.

The murder of Lincoln caused a resurgence of hatred and helped make Reconstruction thoroughly evil. It helped condition the Northern public mind to accept the program mapped out by the industrial clique that had sponsored the war. If most of the things that happened after the war, including Lincoln's murder, were not planned, then this country witnessed a series of coincidences and fortuitive circumstances more remarkable than anything that the Brothers Grimm ever put together.

The Lincoln murder plot was a three cornered affair that was badly bungled. It is always difficult to get two parts of a plan carried out by two independent operators, and this one had three, two of whom were anything but dependable. Beside Lincoln, there were two others scheduled for death that night: Andrew Johnson, the Vice President, and William H. Seward, Secretary of State. The man detailed to take care of Johnson got drunk and staggered about the streets of Washington in a state of terror. Seward's assailant only wounded his man with a Bowie knife and fled. But not only the plot was bungled. If any precautions had been intended for protection of the president, they were also bungled because there weren't any visible to the naked eye; and after the murder, measures taken to apprehend the criminals were also bungled so thoroughly that the bungling must have been planned by experts.

All the strange things that happened, and all the things that strangely didn't happen but should have, constitute good evidence that feet were deliberately being dragged in pursuing the principal suspect, John Wilkes Booth; but details of all this have been brought to light and published in full and need not be repeated here. The point is that it never seemed to occur to anyone at the time to ask two important obvious questions: (1) Who stood to benefit from the crime? and (2) Was he the only one?

Death of both the president and vice president, according to Article II of the Constitution, would have left it up to Congress to select a successor to the president; and nothing could have suited the political power pack better than an opportunity to hand pick Lincoln's successor. The timing would have been perfect, without the bungling.

Thaddeus Stevens of Pennsylvania was the most powerful member of Congress, and the most vengeful foe of the South. Charles Sumner of Massachusetts was the Senate majority leader. Edwin Stanton of Ohio was Secretary of War and his contemptible attitude has already been remarked upon. Did Stanton plan Lincoln's murder, knowing that he would be the choice of Stevens and Sumner as the next president? Were Stevens and Sumner in on the plot? Or did they plan the whole thing and was Stanton acting for them in directing the murder?[1]

For the purpose of the Northern industrial power pack, Stanton would obviously be the ideal president, not during the war, but afterward, for carving up the carcass of the murdered South. The industrialists had needed Lincoln for prosecuting the war, which required skillful political maneuvering, and Lincoln knew how to do that better than anyone else at the time. His theory was just the thing on which to run the war, but now just the opposite was needed. Lincoln, too, had made himself too great in the eyes of the Northern people. He had achieved his ambition. Great power and influence had come into his hands, and the tight clique that had backed him could no longer trust him. He had nothing more to gain by carrying out the War Party's plan for extinction of the South. He had outgrown his usefulness. A butcher like Stanton was needed now.

On the other hand, Lincoln would have had little to gain by stubbornly opposing the War Party's ultimate plans. He knew their power and how to adapt himself to circumstances. He could be flexible, talk ambiguously, hold back and wait until he saw how things were going before making his move, but for the power pack it would be too risky to depend on him any longer. Lincoln wanted to maintain his saintly image and had been able to do so up to then, but the plans of Stevens and Sumner were even more savage than war, and they wanted somebody who would unquestionably go all the way with them. Stanton was already their man and there was no question about what he would do. To get him, both Lincoln and Johnson had to go, and also Seward who was popular and might have come forward as a possible choice of the majority in Congress.

As it turned out, the War Party would have been smart to let well enough alone and take their chances on forcing Lincoln to keep on going along with them; but they had so much at stake that they went for King, Cawdor, Glamis all. The inexcusable bungling that let Andrew Johnson in for the top spot turned out to be a disaster for them. It was foolish for the plotters, who wanted three people assassinated simultaneously, to turn the job over to a half crazy star of the stage

who would hire clumsy amateurs for the minor roles so that
his own performance would stand out that much brighter,
but then would ham it up unnecessarily and break his leg.
But the plotters had to employ the best they could get.
There weren't too many men who could be induced to press
the muzzle of a pistol against the head of another and cooly
squeeze the trigger.

Everything fits together like the pieces of a jig saw puzzle.
No conclusions exclude any of the facts. No sane Southerner would have done away with Lincoln and Johnson and
left the choice of a new president up to a Congress dominated by the South's bitterest and most unscrupulous enemies. And if any Southerner had planned the job, Stanton
would surely have been a sure thing for one of the victims.
That he was in on the crime is strongly indicated by the
trial of the accused assassins and accessories. It was just
the sort of thing a frustrated despot would put on to revenge
himself against the clowns who had fouled up their assign-
ment and cost him the kingdom. Stanton had no love for
Lincoln, or for anyone except Stanton, and his treatment of
the accused was not for punishment, because they had not
been convicted. (Stanton was a lawyer!) He designed the
canvas hoods that were pulled over their heads during their
trial, and the solid bar type manacles that were fastened
upon their wrists.

That the trial was by a military commission roused the ire
of Attorney General Bates, but Stanton had to keep tight
control over the proceedings to prevent too much truth from
leaking out. Not since Magna Carta had the rules of justice
been so flagrantly flouted, unless it was at the "bloody as-
sizes" of 1685 under the notorious Jeffrys; and it is unfortunate that our government since then has not seen fit to repudiate the proceedings and reverse the verdicts, especially
that of the herois Dr. Mudd. The vilest criminals today are
turned loose upon the public for the slightest error on the
part of the prosecution, yet the abuses perpetrated by Stanton have been allowed to reek upon the record for more than
a century.[1]

Underlying the assassination plot was the business of shifting the legal theory of secession. Almost four years before, on July 22, 1861, the day after the First Battle of Manassas (Bull Run) the Crittendon Resolutions passed the House of Representatives with only two dissenting votes, and on the 23rd, the Senate passed the same resolution with only five dissenters. The Senate resolution was proposed by Senator Andrew Johnson of Tennessee. They declared that the war was not for conquest or for subjugation or for interference with the rights or established customs of the states (meaning that the war was not for abolition of slavery) but only for maintaining the supremacy of the Constitution and the unimpaired rights and equality of the states; and that as soon as these objectives had been accomplished, the war ought to end.

It is amazing that nobody got up and shouted, "Why, these are exactly what the South is fighting for!" The Constitution and States Rights! How can you make enemies of people and go to war with them when they are struggling for the same objectives? It wasn't easy, and took great political skill. If these resolutions could have been presented to the Southern states before hostilities began, before secession especially, the war could have been averted or at least postponed. It is true that there would still have been the problem of the South being dominated by a coalition of Northern and Western States but things would have been moving toward peace.

However, on July 22 and 23, shock waves from the battle were rippling through Congress and the politicians were concerned about public reaction to the disaster. Although the Crittendon Resolutions were almost identical with Lincoln's avowed objectives, he did not feel bound by them because he maintained that dealing with post-war problems was an executive responsibility and that Congress had no right to interfere. (Later he was persuaded otherwise by Stevens.)

Lincoln pulled his first switch a year and a half later with his Emancipation Proclamation which was deliberately designed to "interfere with rights and established customs". He performed other turn-abouts later, one of which was his declaration in 1864 that he would not commit himself to any plan for solving post-war problems. Apparently he was getting ready to be adaptable to shifts in public opinion or possibly to changes in the plans of the controlling political-industrial clique.

He never had a chance to show whether he would have put his original plan into operation and fight for it if Congress opposed him, or slide into the policy that Congress came up with when it convened in 1865. He can be imagined doing anything agreeable to one's appraisal of him, but his death made this mere speculation.

The misfiring of the plot and Johnson's elevation to the presidency caught the War Party off balance, as Congress was not in session. Johnson's policy was much the same as Lincoln's previously announced policy (nobody knows what policy he had in mind at the time of his death) but Johnson had some alterations and additions, and deviated from the Resolutions he had sponsored in July 1861. Rights to property would be unimpaired except that slaves would be free although Negroes would have no part in the plan. Blanket amnesty would be granted, but only to the small farmers and trades people. They would form the new state governments. The old "ruling class", wealthy slave owners and people of influence under the old regime would be disfranchised and would have to apply individually to him personally for restoration of citizenship.

Lincoln had in mind suggesting to the states after the war, that Negroes be admitted to some kind of limited suffrage. He did not believe that they should hold office or serve on juries. Both he and Johnson held that the president could, by executive order, pardon and restore citizenship to those who had taken up arms against the federal government, and could condition this upon an oath of allegiance to the Constitution. (The president had the right to pardon convicted criminals, why not ex-Confederates, assuming, of course, that they were guilty of anything. And didn't we just have an instance of a president pardoning an ex-president before any charges were drawn up against him?) But the indigestible part of Lincoln demanding an oath of allegiance to the Constitution was that he himself had violated the Constitution so flagrantly that, in terms of his own attitude, such an oath would mean little. Another twist in his attitude was that he didn't want a new state government in Virginia because he wanted the old government back again so that "the same government that took it (the state) out of the Union could bring it back"; but he had maintained that Virginia had never been out of the Union.

Without waiting for Congress, Johnson issued blanket amnesty and restored citizenship to the "small people" so that they could get busy and form their state governments out of their own ranks. The others, members of his hated "upper class" would have to humble themselves and beg for restoration. Now ruined, they had no choice, and it gratified the meanness of his nature to humiliate those who had held him in low esteem.

But while Johnson was busy handling applications for pardon, and telling about his rise from poverty the leaders of Congress were busy developing plans to supersede his executive orders. They had no intention of recognizing the voting rights he was granting to Confederates, little or big, or recognizing the state governments being set up by them. The Crittendon Resolutions were no good any more. Neither was the concept of an indestructible Union. Preserve the Union? Stevens & Co. would make a new one. Out the window went the idea that Congress had no power to regulate suffrage, no matter what the Constitution might say about that being distinctly a state prerogative. It was therefore with many pretzel-shaped thought processes that Congress produced twin theories on the status of the Confederate states, one the House theory, one the Senate theory.

The Senate theory presupposed that the Confederate states had destroyed themselves and abdicated their Constitutional rights, that their state governments had ceased to exist, all institutions and property rights within them having been thereby abolished. There was no law in the former Confederacy, and Congress could enact such laws as it saw fit for the people there, its power to do so limited only by the Declaration of Independence as the supreme law of the land, the Constitution having no provision for that kind of emergency. Here was another kink in their thinking: the Declaration of Independence clearly justifies secession, "That whenever any form of government becomes destructive of these ends (life, liberty and the pursuit of happiness) it is the right of the people to alter or abolish it.....when a long train of abuses and usurpations.....design to reduce them under absolute despotism.....it is their duty to throw off such government....."

The magnanimous spirit responsible for this plan was that of Charles Sumner, but before deciding that he had been hit too hard on the head by the man with a cane, one should consider the plan evolved in the House of Representatives.[1]

Supposedly the more democratic of the two legislative bodies, the House did a "one-up" on the Senate. It regarded the former Confederacy as territory acquired by conquest, subject to no laws except the laws of war, and that war makes its own laws. White Southerners had no rights at all and were entirely at the mercy of Congress whose power was absolute, unlimited by either the Constitution or the Declaration of Independence or anything else. All land and possessions were to be confiscated and held by the federal government to cover the cost of the war including damage to "loyal" citizens and to pay the pensions for Northern soldiers and their families, or to be divided up in 40 acre plats and parcelled out to freed slaves, with a mule thrown in. The Rebels were to be exterminated or exiled and replaced with a new population, while Southern Negroes were to be immediately enfranchised. Never mind that this seems unbelievable. It is on record.[1]

The House plan was the creation of Representative Thaddeus Stevens of Pennsylvania, the most powerful politician in Washington and evil genius of the Northern Power Pack, or War Party, call it what you will. Naturally, he became known in the South as the "Father of Reconstruction".

Both plans declared all Southern whites to be foreigners, but conferred immediate full citizenship on all Southern Negroes but not on Northern Negroes who were denied the franchise in Stevens' own state, as well as in most of the other states. All the plans, Lincoln's and Johnson's included, attainted all Southern whites as traitors, but never questioned if any Southern Negroes, slave or free, had also been guilty of "treason" as principals or accessories. So one was white with guilt and black with innocence, by federal legislative act and without trial.[2]

The most obvious and remarkable feature of the Stevens-Sumner plan, which would have embarrassed them if they had been embarrassable was its failure to fit a lot of facts that went before, Tennessee, for instance. When the 11 Southern states seceded, 21 Southern senators resigned. One retained his seat for more than a year after his state went out of the Union and went out, incidentally, by an overwhelming margin. That senator was Andrew Johnson of Tennessee, who continued to participate in all legislative functions just as he had always done, serving on committees, arguing for and against bills, and voting. He introduced the Senate version of the Crittendon Resolutions. Under the Stevens-Sumner theory he was a foreigner representing a foreign nation, serving illegally in the Senate.

This ought to be of considerable interest today because if the Supreme Court endorses the Stevens-Sumner theory, wouldn't a lot of legislation have to be invalidated, and court decisions based on laws passed while Johnson participated in their passage have to be reversed? On the other hand, if the Supreme Court upholds the Lincoln-Johnson theory, wouldn't everything done by Congress during the Reconstruction period have to be thrown out including amendments to the Constitution and decisions based on them since? How could any court uphold BOTH Stevens-Sumner and Lincoln-Johnson?

The Lincoln-Johnson theory had great trouble trying to crawl under cover of the Constitution, and there was no way it could make it. Its original premise was wrong: that the Union existed before the states and was indestructible. The Union was created by the Constitution and the Constitution was created by the states; and some of the states provided for the division of the Union by retaining the right to withdraw if they didn't like what they had created, (Virginia was one.)

Lincoln also claimed that his violations of the Constitution were for the purpose of "preserving the Union"; but how could the Union be preserved without the Constitution? Which created this union. It was the Union's heart and soul and backbone. We swear allegiance to the Constitution, not to the Union, and so did Lincoln. It is not an idle oath. Lincoln, the champion of the Union, tore up the Constitution; Garrison, champion of abolition, burned it in public; the Confederates took it with them when they "brought forth upon this continent a new nation".

The bald concept of "union" is a shallow one. Union cannot be forced upon incompatible components. Internal stress can blast apart the strongest structure. What the Constitutional Convention created was a Republic, a Democratic Republic but not a Democracy. A democracy is a football game without any rules. It is the Constitution that establishes the rules, and the rules should not be changed in the middle of a game. The edifice that our Constitution erected has its foundation on the ground but is raised above it. A Republic is difficult to maintain against the greed and ambition of selfish individuals and groups. Its administration requires an uncommon degree of ability and fidelity.

It might be well to remember that the Roman republic was destroyed by Sulla who murdered the masters of 10,000 slaves and then enfranchised the slaves to gain power over his country. If less were said about WHY Rome fell and more about HOW the Republic was destroyed, we could learn more from our history books.

Charles Sumner's plan was an attempt to be half way in and half way out of the Constitution. Sumner knew that the Constitution wouldn't let him do what he wanted to do, but he felt that he had to have some written justification for his plan, so he fell back on the Declaration of Independence. He did think that if Congress reinstated or created any new states, Congress would be bound to guarantee such states a republican form of government.

Thaddeus Stevens considered the Constitution only a "scrap of parchment", but in trying NOT to be constitutional, he was. His theory that the Confederacy was foreign territory admitted that it could only have become so by having the constitutional right to secede and make itself a foreign nation. Stevens' theory was an admission that the war was an act of aggression on the part of the federal government, but he probably could not have cared less.

It was Stevens' plan that was adopted in its entirety, implemented by laws extending the Freedmen's Bureau, the Civil Rights Act, and the activities of the Loyal League. All the volunteers and vultures, home grown and imported, Scalywags, Carpetbaggers, were encouraged to grab whatever the marauders had overlooked during the war. The plan insisted on full Negro suffrage, based on the premise that the Negroes so hated their former masters and all white Southerners and would be so grateful to the Republican Party for their freedom that they would forever vote to keep the Republican Party in power and, incidentally keep the Stevens Power Pack forever in control of the Republican Party. However, if the Negroes didn't respond in this way, Stevens had plans to see to it that they jolly well did so.[1]

It seems now that the Lincoln-Johnson contention that restoration of citizenship was exclusively an executive prerogative is rejected. The Congress, not the president, has restored citizenship to General Lee whose application was "lost sight of" for over a century, and also to Jefferson Davis who never applied at all. General Lee believed that army officers ought not to be in politics and politics ought not to be in the army. Seldom did he say anything that had political implications though he was frequently consulted by friends during the time Southerners were "aliens", but when he did speak, he made more sense than all the politicians. He said, "If the Union was paramount, and the secession of a state was wrong, then the exclusion of a state by the federal government is just as wrong."

The cards were face up now on the table for all who wanted to see, but it is still claimed by some that the war was brought on by a few of the South's slaveholding "oligarchy" to perpetuate slavery because their dominant position was founded upon it. Some still say that Southern legislatures under the thumb of the slaveholding minority voted for secession despite the pro-Union sentiments of the majority and that popular votes taken later to approve secession were conducted under the threat of Confederate bayonets. This is ridiculous. It is true that there was much pro-Union sentiment in the South. Most people were reluctant to sever the bonds, but from the moment when Lincoln called for troops to "put down the rebellion", such pro-Union sentiment as had survived up to then evaporated almost entirely.

That a small oligarchy dominated the South against the will of the people is repudiated by the attitude of Stevens himself in 1866. As the elections that year approached, he feared that if Johnson obtained a majority in the House, Southern representatives might be seated in both houses and, joining forces with "copperhead" Northern Democrats, nullify the 13th amendment, destroy the Freedmen's Bureau and the Civil Rights law, remove occupation troops from the South and leave the "loyalist" minority and the Negroes at the mercy of a hostile populace, (besides, of course, destroying the power of the Republican Party.) So, after four years of war, the pro-Unionists of the South were greatly in the minority, having lost their majority status, while the majority that had been browbeaten by the "oligarchy" were willing to re-instate their browbeaters.

However, if there had ever been any means by which the South could have obtained a majority in both Houses, there would have been no need for secession. Anything that might have headed off the growing power of the radical Republican Party of which Stevens was the leader, would have averted secession, but the idea that the South was fighting for slavery has become so fixed in most minds that contrary ideas are accorded scant attention. The truth is that with a balanced power structure, the Union would have survived intact, strong, prosperous and progressive. The efforts of the abolitionists alone could never have brought on war.

CHAPTER XXVI:

THE DESPOT'S HEEL

If there was still any doubt about the intentions of the Northern War Party, it disappeared in the war's aftermath. Congress was not in session when Johnson stepped into Lincoln's shoes, and this may have been an advantage to the plotters and planners. They had some broad outlines on their mental blackboards, no doubt, but there were no well greased wheels ready to whirr at the touch of a button. The time lag gave them a chance to get organized with a plan as soon as congress convened.

Johnson had gone ahead granting amnesty and helping state governments get back into business, but when representatives of these states came to Washington after having been duly elected by Johnson's re-enfranchised "little people", Congress refused to seat them and sent them home. Steered by the powerful machine of Stevens and Sumner, Congress then went about the business of taking the reins of government out of the hands of the president. Congress passed laws, Johnson vetoed them, and Congress passed them over the veto.

These laws divided the former Confederacy into five military districts and clothed the commanders of each with almost unlimited power. They also extended the powers of the Freedmen's Bureau which was established in the first place as an insult to the white people in that its purpose was avowedly to "protect" the Negroes from them. It was dominated by the most unscrupulous politicians the South had ever seen, and local offices were run mostly by men with little or no ability and even less good will.

The military commander of a district used his absolute power to promote the Bureau in its efforts to coerce Negroes. He could set up military tribunals for the trial of anyone, suspend the powers of police and local civil officials and do just about anything that an army of occupation in a hostile foreign country could do. Some loyal Negroes went to their white people and asked what they should do, and often the advice they got, for their own protection, was to go ahead and vote Republican. Negroes were being urged not to live in the old houses the whites had provided for them before the war, and not to work for their former masters; but the Bureau had made so many rules and regulations that few white people could afford to hire Negroes anyway. Political orators exhorted Negroes to commit arson and even murder. That there was not more violence shows that there was still much good will between the races.

The Union League got organized in the North during the war to pump up patriotism among those who were showing a diminishing desire to be up and about the Lord's work. During the Reconstruction era, the Freedmen's Bureau promoted the Union League among Negroes in the South for political purposes, along with the Loyalty Leagues. They were secret societies and were used to pressure Negroes into voting Republican and becoming politically active under the corrupt political leaders. The pressure exerted upon them was enormous. That these organizations had to go to such extremes to force the Negroes into line is good evidence that a great number of Negroes still wanted to be loyal to their old white friends. Those who were reluctant to go along with the mob were harangued, ridiculed, threatened and ostracised by those under the thumb of the invaders. The most stubborn ones were even excluded from their church, and sometimes found that their wives and sweethearts had been urged to turn against them. Some of the more defiant were beaten and some murdered. The worst types of Negroes and whites were employed in this effort to wipe out all opposition to the nation's dominant political party.[1]

At the war's end, Southern whites had a warm feeling of gratitude toward Negroes who were loyal during the hostilities, but the new Northern policy was designed to destroy all that and give the Negro as ugly an image as possible. If prospects were dim for the ex-Confederate soldier, they were even dimmer for the ex-slave. The slaves had been entirely dependent upon their masters for everything. Those who had been employed by the more prosperous planters, or those in close contact with the white family, enjoyed a real sense of security. Even the free Negroes depended wholly on the whites for the sale of their products or services. Now all that was gone. The whites had nothing themselves, and they were faced with the bewildering problem of how to provide bare necessities. The Negroes had never known that problem because subsistence had always been a matte of course. In spite of being free, and being, supposedly, cared for by the Freedmen's Bureau, they were more bewildered than the whites.

It is not true that the Negroes had won their freedom, as is so often said, or even that their freedom had been won for them. They were still just as dependent upon whites as they ever were, and they found, when the Bureau took over, that they had only changed their masters and not for the better. The dream of freedom was the dream of the abolitionists, not the dream of the Negroes and the conditions that followed the war were far from being a dream. The slaves had all heard about freedom, and were acquainted with free Negroes and knew what their lot was like. Was it such as to inspire desperate efforts to acquire the same? And what was the lot of Negroes in the North? Would Southern Negroes want THAT, if they knew the facts?

The more imaginative, however, must have gotten the idea that the freedom the abolitionists talked about was something different, something not of this world, and they must have wondered in what form it would come. Perhaps those given to dreaming expected a figure in radiant white garments to descend out of a cloud with trumpets and announce that henceforth they would be free from all worries; but even to the practical minded, it must have come as a letdown just to be told in simple terms, "You are free now. I am no longer your master. There is nothing I can do for you any more". Many must have said to themselves, "Massa ain't hisself. The war done made a ole man outen him".

The truth is that freedom had been forced upon the slaves; or it might be said that they had been thrown out of work by the enforced failure of their employers. Being out of work is one form of freedom. When there is no one to say, "Come on, Sam. Get moving", the worker may have had a sense of freedom but perhaps it was more like a feeling of having been abandoned.

Confusion existed because there had been no preparation for freedom. Many slaves immediately walked off the old home place to get something for nothing at the Freedmen's Bureau. Glowing promises were being made there, land and mules and equipment that had been confiscated for the use of ex-slaves, and the prospect of becoming a property owner was an attractive one. But some came to their ex-masters and asked advice, and found that their ex-masters had no advice to give themselves. Some simply said, "Go ahead and work the land for what you can get out of it"; and it was at this point that share cropping became an institution. Whites had land but nothing else, Negroes had nothing but ability to work. A mutual profit sharing arrangement resulted. It proved successful for many years, on the whole an equitable practice, and it did much to save the South.

The power nucleus in Congress that had pushed through the laws giving Southern Negroes the vote had no intention of allowing them to use it according to the dictates of their own individual conscience and judgement. That was not the reason they had been enfranchised in place of the disfranchised whites. This new big black bloc of votes would be dominated by SS troops (Stevens-Sumner) to perpetuate their control of the Republican Party and to perpetuate the Republican Party in control of the government. Negroes would be herded to the polls and forced to vote as instructed.

To do this, an organization was needed, a ruthless organization with a chain of command from the top down to the humblest members. To carry out orders with no questions asked, individuals were recruited who had always been willing to live by any means that did not require earning daily bread by the sweat of the brow. They were the loud talkers, the glib promisers, better at borrowing than at repaying, who feared force but loved to use it when they could. They were Negroes that other Negroes would not have trusted, left to themselves, and there were some whites that other whites held in special contempt. These were the ones from both races that were put up for election and appointment to public office, the ones who would squander what was left of the South's resources.

As the Bureau and the Leagues gained wider control over the Negro population amid the wreckage of the old way of life, there began to grow an estrangement between the two races that had not been there before. It did not come about spontaneously on the part of either, nor during the privations of war time. It was deliberately fomented at the end of the Confederacy's armed resistance, by the Bureau and the Leagues. It was a massive effort, supported by the apathy of the Northern public, who never found out how evil the program was, although the evidence was plainly visible. The public mind, however, had been conditioned not to look, only to accept what came through the propaganda channels.

The most notorious example of what was coming through the propaganda channels was the Hays-Hawley letter of September 7, 1874. U.S.Senator Joseph Hawley of Connecticut wanted some inflamatory anti-Southern material to boost his campaign for re-election. He wrote to Representative Charles Hays of Alabama, a particularly obnoxious scalywag, asking for incidents of outrages committed by white Southerners. Hays gave him details of 13 horrible crimes of beatings, riots, murders, burnings, and tortures, all of which, Hays stated, had occurred within his personal observation. Hawley published these in full and the press gave them wide coverage. They created a nation wide sensation. The public avidly devoured them all without question. President Grant alerted federal troops in Alabama to be ready to suppress any fresh outrages. The New York Tribune sent a special correspondent to Alabama to investigate. He interviewed all the people who were supposed to have been beaten, tortured, burned, murdered or to have participated in riots. His report declared that every charge was a deliberate lie, known by Hays to have been so. The New York Tribune was never known to have been a friend of the South, for which all the more credit is due its staff for their loyalty to truth. It did not, however, recondition the Northern public mind.[1]

It had been just as hard for anybody in the South to figure out what was going on. No one issued a book of rules. In fact, there weren't any rules. Federal officials set themselves up, issued edicts and the troops marched in to enforce them. The people were under a totalitarian government, and nobody knew what the next move would be. The whites were without money, many without the property they had before the war, and all were without citizenship. The Negroes had been given citizenship but didn't know what to do with it. The Freedmen's Bureau and the Leagues would show them what to do with it and see that they did it. The Negroes were trapped in a situation not of their making or of their own desire. A swarm of strangers whom they didn't understand had moved in between them and the white folks they had always depended on. The lazy ones, the greedy ones, and the ones with delusions of grandeur and wild ambitions for power delighted in carrying out the programs of the Bureau; but at the height of their glory, when they felt themselves firmly entrenched, and when conditions were intolerable for people anxious for honest government and prosperous economy, a new and unique organization suddenly came into existence and virtually saved the South.

It may come as strange news to some that one reason the Ku Klux Klan was organized was to end the oppression of Negroes by the Freedmen's Bureau and its stooges, the Loyalty Leagues, the Scalywags and Carpetbaggers. The Klan's objective was to end violence, not to add to it, and to end the flagrant corruption that was bleeding the section to death. The Negroes were being re-enslaved by the very people claiming to be their liberators. The Klan saved the Negroes as well as the whites.

The Klan's origin is a little obscure, but it apparently started out as a student club with no thought of involvement in politics. There were no uniforms or military regulations, only officers with fantastic titles like Grand Dragon, Grand Kleagle, etc., just the sort of thing college boys would go for. General Nathan Bedford Forrest is generally credited with organizing the Klan together with several other organizations into an effective political force. Who dreamed up the white robes and hoods and how extensively they were used, no one seems to know, but it is impossible, since the Birth of a Nation, to imagine a Klansman without a tall, pointed hood and flowing white robes. The original members formed themselves into groups that rode out at night to the homes of selected persons, not always Negroes by any means. They usually found a single visit and a simple suggestion was all that was necessary. Their efforts met with instant success.

People who have never heard the thunder of approaching hoof beats in force can't imagine what an awesome sound it can be at midnight in a silent rural area. One who was suddenly awakened to find himself surrounded by excessively tall horsemen would very likely take seriously a suggestion to pick out some other location or method of making a living. The first to receive such a visit would be sure to spread exaggerated accounts of the experience, and in rural areas, such news would travel fast. Others would then think that they might be scheduled for a similar visit and resign from politics without being invited to do so.

How much violence was committed by the original Klan would be impossible to estimate. Obviously, the Klan kept no records. It is reasonable to suppose, however, that these first members were not guilty of very much if any, almost certainly no wanton violence. They were ex-Confederate soldiers, led by ex-Confederate officers, public spirited men used to positions of command and trained in the disciplines of leadership. Besides, they could see that their methods were effective without use of force. It is believed that the original Klan lasted less than three years, and disbanded when it had accomplished its objective. The trouble was that other men with less lofty objectives, seeing how effective such techniques could be, got together in gangs and set out for personal gain and revenge. The outrages charged to the Ku Klux Klan could have been committed by anybody for any purpose, or not committed at all. In any event, the organization that got going in the 1920's and called itself the Ku Klux Klan had not the remotest connection with the original, but that is another story.

CHAPTER XXVII:

WHAT IF IT HAD MISFIRED?

Any comparison between what did happen and what might
have happened involves a crystal ball; but it could give some
perspective to the parade of events to speculate on what
Abraham Lincoln might have done if he had not taken in a
matinee on that Good Friday, or if Booth's derringer had
misfired.

Lincoln would certainly not have let matters come to a
show-down between his own principles and the Stevens-
Sumner group. He was too clever a politician and his principles were too flexible. He was jealous of his prerogatives,
especially against encroachment by the military, and he had
often reminded his generals not to make any political commitments in occupied areas or in dealing with opposing generals, but he was wary about being too strict with political
generals like Butler, as mentioned before. On the delicate
subject of whether the president or congress should handle
the post-war problem of restoring the seceding states to full
membership in the Union, he was in a vulnerable position,
but he would have forseen what the War Party's attitude
was going to be. How would he have avoided a confrontation?

Historically, political leaders lose their popularity after a
war, and Lincoln might not have been an exception. It was
the assassination that gave him a saintly image, coming at
the height of a public acclaim that would probably have
been temporary. When the euphoria flattened out, he would
have become the target of dissatisfied political groups. He
would have been quick to see, if he had not already seen,
that the Crittendon Resolutions wouldn't stick, and that the
War Party had too much control in congress for him to hold
out too firmly against them. He might have tried an oblique
attack of some kind, but for what purpose? He was up
against a determined and ruthless group that would stop at
nothing (and did indeed stop at nothing; they murdered

him).

If it had been bad politics for Lincoln to curb Stanton during the war, how much worse would it have been to tackle him afterward when his backers, Stevens' power nucleus, were more firmly in control? Certainly Lincoln would never have allowed his relations with Congress to deteriorate so far that laws would be necessary to restrict his authority. Congress even forbade Johnson, the Commander-in-Chief of the armed forces, to issue orders directly to his generals. All orders had to go through the General of the Army who could not be ordered away from Washington without his own consent. That was angry legislation, a slap in the President's face, and it took a lot of political pressure to get Congress to pass such a law and also the Tenure of Office Act forbidding the President to dismiss an appointee who had been confirmed by the Senate unless Congress concurred in the dismissal. That was, of course, an attempt to keep Johnson from firing Stanton. Lincoln would have avoided getting into that kind of corner no matter what he had to do.

It can be assumed that Stevens and Sumner would have set about the same kind of reconstruction program as they did even though, without the assassination they would not have had an aroused Northern public to count on for support, and Lincoln might have won some concessions with his "malice toward none" speeches, but how far would he dare go, and what was to be gained by taking a risk? The War Party had its objectives in its grip and was not about to let go. Lincoln had kow-towed to Stevens during the war. Against such a determined and ruthless organization, a clever politician would have crawled into bed with Stevens and Sumner under cover of Biblical quotations and declarations of high purpose. It should not be hard to imagine Lincoln doing just that.

The bull-headed Johnson, however, met matters head on, went ahead and booted Stanton out in defiance of the Tenure of Office Act, and was impeached by the Reconstructionists. He was tried by the Senate with B.F. (Beast) Butler as judge, and was acquitted by one vote.

One vote or a dozen, the result of the trial was a decisive blow to the "Down-with-the-white-South" phalanx. Stanton was out, and drunken old mean-spirited Johnson, the poor man's friend, had thrown a monkey wrench into Big Industry's political machinery and saved the South, or what was left of it. It destroyed him politically and amounted to self sacrifice but not an act of unselfish sacrifice. Johnson was just compulsively stubborn, and he never had a chance at a second term anyway. He was soon out of politics. General Grant, the "savior of the country" was elected to succeed him and muddled through eight years of an administration that almost ruined the country he had supposedly saved. The financial panic of 1873 was the result of corruption in high finance and politics, and was followed by one of the country's worst depressions, though that was not entirely Grant's fault. Lincoln's "phony money", the greenbacks with which he financed the war really caused it. Grant vetoed Congress' attempt to issue more greenbacks. In spite of the record, attempts were made to give Grant a third term. They failed.

In the election of 1876, Republican Rutherford B. Hayes and Democrat Samuel Tilden were close, though Tilden had the popular vote majority. A deal was made to swing the electoral votes of several Southern states to Hayes in return for a promise that all remaining federal troops would be removed from Southern soil. It was a deal that Hayes and his party were glad to accept. (When the presidency is within reach, a politician will snap at it like a seal at a herring.) Hayes was chiefly noted for repairing some of the Grant administration blunders.

By this time, most of the steam had escaped from the wrecking party launched by Thaddeus Stevens and Charles Sumner. Stevens had died in 1868, Sumner in 1874. Jefferson Davis, imprisoned in Fortress Monroe for two years without being charged, was finally indicted and the indictment promptly quashed. The government did not dare bring him to trial because too many embarrassing and politically dangerous results might have flowed from the wrong kind of verdict. By then too, the Ku Klux Klan had discouraged the worst of the thieving politicians, and some shifting of public attention to other matters in the North permitted some of the former Southern leaders who had not been killed or completely ruined, to regain their influence.

Political conditions in the South could not be considered very good, but they were a big improvement over what had been imposed upon the people there by Stevens and Sumner. The Republican Party had permitted this clique of psychopathic despots to give it such a repulsive image that it never recovered in the South, much even to the later disadvantage of the South itself. Blind adherence to a single party regardless of the issues robbed the South of the political flexibility needed to negotiate for worthwhile objectives; but at least, the "liberators" were gone. So were many Southerners, bereft of home and means of livelihood, forced into exile from the land they loved and had fought for with all their resources.

Compare this post-war policy with the policy adopted by our country following World War II which strengthened our enemies and enabled them to recover prosperity faster than our allies. Russia, never a real ally, has, and with our tacit approval, greatly enlarged its domain at the expense of nations friendly to us. We aided many enemy nations in the restoration of war damaged property, but none of that after the "Civil War". The South was plundered and then saddled with a huge debt to the federal government.

CHAPTER XXVIII:

THE LIBERATORS LEAVE

The Reconstruction era lasted eleven years, and its effects were all bad. At the end, the Republicans took the presidential victory they had bought from the Southern Democrats, and left. The "Liberators" abandoned the impoverished Negroes and left them to fall back on the impoverished whites for life's necessities. The country had been picked clean, and the terms for "re-entering the Union" to which the captive legislatures had agreed under the bayonets of occupation troops would leave the South burdened with debts for a hundred years, debts paid into the federal treasury unto the last penny while debts of foreign nations, even hostile nations, were being forgiven or reduced to mere tokens.[1]

Propagandists promptly promoted the popular belief that no conquered people had ever been shown such leniency, but historian Charles Francis Adams wrote that he could not recall any case where the vanquished party had a heavier fine inflicted upon it, and certainly no occasion in history when recently enfranchised slaves had full legislative power given them over their former masters. Adams considered Southern slaves worth about three billion dollars which, plus 800 million dollars toward paying the pension bill (enemy pensions) made the Southern indemnity equal to the indemnity imposed upon the French by the Germans after the War of 1870. The French lost Alsace Lorraine and were assessed a billion dollars cash, but war damage was nothing compared with devastation of the South, and the French population was six or eight times that of the South, the white South, that is. The whites paid the taxes and bore the cost of the indemnity. Negroes would pay but little taxes for many years. It seems worth while asking why the "enormous" reparations enforced by Germany were considered the "scandal of the 19th century".[2]

The politicians who had been concerned about the Negroes when the Negroes were not begging for their help, now turned their attention to building for themselves more rail-roads, mills, ships, mansions, office building, factories, banks and bicycles with big front wheels. They needed more people to work for them at minimum wages, so they combed the slums of Europe in the economically depressed countries for the poorest people they could find, desperate people who would work for a few cents a day. They even put up a plaque in New York Harbor inscribed with a plea for the nations of the world to send over more cheap help.

Why did Northern industrialists import Europeans when there were so many Southern Negroes who, they supposed, were grateful for the freedom conferred on them by these Northern politicians and would be willing and even eager to go north and work? If Northerners believed what they said about equality couldn't they have trained Negroes more quickly than aliens and put them to work in their factories and offices, especially in Pennsylvania and Massachusetts, home states of Stevens and Sumner? Here was a chance to establish "human rights" without in-human means, but if ever a word escaped the lips of these two "freedom" champions on the subject of bringing Negroes out of the darkness of Southern oppression into the enlightenment of Northern equality, there was nobody around to hear it.

And where were the zealots who had defied the fugitive slave laws and made such a big item for the history books out of the "underground railroad"? Here was a chance to make a piker out of Harriet Tubman with her paltry 300 Negroes smuggled from the chains of Southern slavery into the happy estate of Northern freedom. A thousand Harriet Tubmans could have brought three thousand Negroes each from poverty into industrial prosperity, and still have supplied only a fraction of the number of people needed by the man-hungry machine age.[1]

Economic conditions in the South were desperate, on the farms and in the cities. In the spring of 1869, two old ships came into the Gosport, Virginia's Navy Yard to be altered and fitted out, and men came running to the yard, said one observer, as though all nearby Portsmouth was on fire. About 300 men were taken on, many of them on the verge of starvation. Throughout the South, the poorest of people on a diet of hog and hominy barely managed to stave off starvation but not pellagra and hook worm; but during the years from 1861 to 1870, two million three hundred thousand immigrants were admitted into the United States, and nearly three million more before 1880.[1]

The "Liberators" left a land of ashes and ruin, and a future that was far off and for many would never be. The young men, the dreamers of dreams, who plan and build with hope,- where were they? How appraise the loss of young men whose potential value to the future could only be guessed at by the manner of their death? How calculate the value of the fine old homes destroyed and those that would stand empty until they died of decay? And the once productive plantations that would grow up to weeds, brush and crooked pines?

To the economic collapse that would have followed uncompensated emancipation, was now added the war's destruction, and the incalculable impairment during Reconstruction that could have healed physical wounds. The violence done to relationships between whites and Negroes by the vengeful Bureau and the Leagues could not be measured in money or any other medium.

The Republican Party would undergo changes over the years, as would the Democratic Party also, but the South would remain a mere appendage to this day, not a vital part of the Union on a par with the other states. A century of poverty in the South followed the war and Southern political influence remained almost at zero. Discriminatory legislation is still enacted and upheld by federal courts, and legislation desired by a greedy few is opposed in vain by Southern Congressmen and Senators.

The Union of Sovereign States, each state deriving its powers from its own people, and the federal government having only those powers granted it by the states, ended when Lincoln was allowed to eviscerate the Constitution. Lincoln did not save the Union, the Union that the delegates founded in 1788. A new Union was created in the 1860's with power over the states, power usurped by deception and maintained by force. It was the promise of continued state sovereignty that induced the people of the 13 former colonies to ratify the Constitution with high hopes for a peaceful future. What if they had known what the future held for their sons and grandsons four score and seven years later?

The enormity of the blunder committed by the people of the North who claimed to be friends of the Negro, has never been fully brought to the attention of a still disinterested public. Here was something happening for the first time in all history, and the Northern public was blind and deaf, and their leaders, both political and spiritual, were entirely uncaring. Four million Negroes were being suddenly projected into full legal citizenship in a land of advanced technology and complex political structure but, completely absorbed in their own narrow interests, the Northern people allowed these new, unprepared and bewildered citizens to fall into the hands of a small group of power seekers who had already demonstrated their determination to exploit them for the evil purpose of destroying a whole section of the country and perpetuating their control over both party and nation. The transition from slave to free man failed to achieve the desired results for the Negro because it was carried out in the wrong spirit.

The fifteen year experience of war and its aftermath could have created a permanent state of guerilla activities. There were Confederate experts in carrying out desperate raids, crippling the efforts of large forces, and some were willing to get going with it. Once started, guerilla warfare increases in violence and destructiveness. It was Lee, not Lincoln, who preserved what was left of the Union. Lincoln died while the Union he talked about preserving was dismembered, torn apart by his own policies. His words about "malice toward none" did nothing to induce his followers to refrain from vengeance. Lee died while the land he loved and fought for was in ruins and turmoil, but his simple plea for patient toil sent his men home in peace and stayed the hands that still would have wielded the sword. Even during the worst of the Reconstruction Lee counselled forbearance and told his officers that the evils of the current administration would not endure. "Truth and honor will prevail", he said.

Maybe it will, but in all the years following the war, the memory of John Brown as a martyr to "human rights" is kept green for the edification of future generations; school children have been reciting "Barbara Frietchie", trampling out the grapes of wrath, and gloating over Sherman's massive pillaging of homes from Atlanta to the sea; and many of the Northern clergy (mostly Protestant clergy, be it said in all frankness) have seemed more concerned with the "martyrdom" of Abraham Lincoln than with the sacrifice made by our Lord and Savior for the salvation of all mankind.

But in the South during the years remaining in that tragic 19th century, there were examples to show that much good will had survived. In every parade of Confederate veterans there was a Negro contingent in gray jackets bedecked with medals, strutting in the early years, tottering in the later ones, but always to the rhythm of lively old tunes like "The Bonny Blue Flag", "The Yellow Rose of Texas", and never without "Dixie" played only as an old time Negro band could play it, with a boy on the drums who knew his sticks, and an ornamented and embellished Negro drum major who could "bust a crowd wide open" with the slightest move.

These medal bedecked Negroes deserved the honors bestowed upon them, even if their names and deeds have been forgotten. The honors were given by men who knew what they did to earn them. They were not awarded for political purposes, but to simple people who only knew that they were doing their duty and never found out how great their performance really was.

Fifty miles below Lexington, Virginia, home of Stonewall Jackson, the Roanoke Fifth Avenue Presbyterian Church still displays a unique stained glass window. It depicts a peaceful scene with a river running through a field and a woods beyond. There is a line of tents in the field, with arms stacked in front, and an inscription beneath "In Memory of Stonewall Jackson" followed by his famous last words, "Let us cross (over) the river and rest in the shade of the trees".

The window was installed some forty years after Jackson's death, by the Reverend L.L.Downing, D.D. originally of Lexington. It has survived lightning strokes and flames.[1] The Reverend Downing and his congregation were Negroes. There is also a bronze statue of Jackson over his grave in the Lexington cemetery, paid for by popular subscription. The first contribution was made by the Negro Baptist Church there whose pastor had been a member of the Sunday School class that Jackson had organized and financed.[2]

In Mississippi on February 11, 1890 an appropriation for a monument to the Confederate dead was being considered. A delegate had just spoken against the bill, when John F. Harris, Negro Republican delegate from Washington County, rose to speak:[3]

"Mr. Speaker! I have arisen here in my place to offer a few words on the bill. I have come from a sick bed...Perhaps it was not prudent for me to come. But, Sir, I could not rest quietly in my room without...contributing...a few remarks of my own. I was sorry to hear the speech of the young gentleman from Marshall County. I am sorry that any son of a soldier should go on record as opposed to the erection of a monument in honor of the brave dead. And, Sir, I am convinced that had he seen what I saw at Seven Pines and in the Seven Days' fighting around Richmond, the battlefield covered with the mangled forms of those who fought for their country and for their country's honor, he would not have made that speech.

"When the news came that the South had been invaded, those men went forth to fight for what they believed, and they made no requests for monuments...But they died, and their virtues should be remembered. Sir, I went with them. I too, wore the gray, the same color my master wore. We stayed four long years, and if that war had gone on till now I would have been there yet... I want to honor those brave men who died for their convictions. When my mother died I was a boy. Who, Sir, then acted the part of a mother to the orphaned slave boy, but my 'old missus'? Were she living now, or could speak to me from those high realms where are gathered the sainted dead, she would tell me to vote for this bill. And, Sir, I shall vote for it. I want it known to all the world that my vote is given in favor of the bill to erect a monument in honor of the Confederate dead".

When the applause died down, the measure passed overwhelmingly, and every Negro member voted "aye".

CHAPTER XXIX:

TECHNOLOGY AND SOCIOLOGY

With the new "enlightened" century, the 20th since the world first heard the message of peace on earth, good will toward men, a coughing, spitting, ill-smelling mechanical creation wracked with internal combustion, got a new revolution going that would profoundly affect the life of every creature on the globe and any that might exist within a radius of a few million miles. Its effect of the South was immediate. Harnessed to agricultural equipment, this foul and noisy package of energy claimed as its first victim the mule, up to that time the farmer's most efficient source of power. But the mule ate 365 days a year and only worked 100, and many of those 100 days he was working for himself producing corn for his own consumption. The new device that energized ploughs, reapers, and wagons ate only when working.

Cyrus McCormick's mule drawn "Virginia Reaper", invented in 1836, had been developed to take over some operations that had always been performed manually, and now with the power of many mules available in one chugging unit, more and more of these operations could be performed mechanically and simultaneously. McCormick, single handedly, would have ended slavery peacefully within a few years by making it possible for one white man, sitting down in the shade of a tractor cab, to do what formerly had to be done by many Negroes bending over in the sun.

Negroes had been brought here for 200 years only to grow tobacco and cotton in large quantities on the sub-tropical fields of the Southern states. New technology not only made slavery obsolete, it also made the Negro obsolete. It released large numbers of farm laborers and still would have without the war, but there would have been resources to help prevent hardship. A share in the newly created prosperity would have accrued to the displaced workers in the form of opportunities for employment in the enterprises that the new technology encouraged.

With the new energy, farm equipment got bigger and bigger, more powerful and expensive, too expensive for the small farmer to buy and too efficient for him to compete with. Families that had survived big depressions because they could raise their own food, couldn't survive big mechanization. Big operators, even corporations took over. Small farms were bought up or were abandoned. The surplus labor began to trickle out of the rural South into the big cities of the North. The small trickles became big migrations when the big city politicians, anxious for votes in big blocs, made a bid for minorities, especially Negroes, to come up and enjoy jobs at high wages, and benefits unheard of at public expense.

There were jobs but not nearly enough of them to fulfill the big promises of the political pied pipers, and the new immigrants packed themselves into "low rent" areas, accepted of necessity the handouts, and brought up their children in a vastly different environment. They became a made-to-order audience for "promising" oratory and ideal material with which the politically ambitious could get a "social revolution" going, with "equality", not excellence, as the ostensible goal but also with the plus of promised special privileges. Accordingly, and having much in common with the first attempt, a big black bloc of votes was organized, but this would be a new story with too many involvements for discussion here.

But the South remains politically where it was when the war ended in 1865. The war settled no questions, resolved no issues, not even the issue of secession, in principle. It merely prevented by force the secession of certain states at that time. The big issue raised by George Mason at the Constitutional Convention of 1788 is still what it was, a weakness in the structure, a built-in stress, and while it exists the South will be a second rate section, dominated by a cohesive majority of Northern states, and outvoted on all matters vital to internal Southern interests. There is even a little publicized but organized effort to abolish entirely the identity of all states and substitute ten "regions" (already set up) for the 50 states, with such absurd jurisdictional divisions as one that would have the affairs of Virginia and some other Southern states administered from Philadelphia. Thus, while the old problems remain with us, we are adding new ones; but that too is another story.

There are some academic questions raised by these problems that are worth thinking about. If, at the Constitutional Convention, Virginia had held out for the abolition of slavery and for the two-thirds majority voting rule on the enactment of import duties, and had refused to join the Union unless these two amendments were adopted, what would have happened?

The seven Northern colonies at that time had a two-thirds majority of the total white population of the country in 1790. Tactical difficulties usually would have made it impractical to muster a two-thirds vote on that basis in the House and impossible in the Senate, and both sides would probably have been cautious about going to extremes if the Virginia amendments had been accepted.

The amendment abolishing slavery would have been a different thing. Many Southerners wanted an end to slavery because there were nearly three-quarters of a million Negroes in the South who, with better living conditions, better nutrition and sanitation, were multiplying rapidly. People foresaw problems in the future with two such deeply dissimilar races living together under the same laws and customs. As people usually do, however, people were basing their ideas on the assumption that economic conditions would remain static. No one could then foresee the onset of the Industrial Revolution and the pressures it would bring for multiplication of cotton production. Even Northerners went South and became Southern planters and, later, loyal Confederates.

As manufacturing expanded in the North and McCormack's

Virginia Reaper opened up the West, Europeans were imported to work as mill hands in New England or as farmers in the West, but Europeans could not have been induced to work as field hands in Southern fields, and there were no means whereby Africans could have been induced to ship out voluntarily, pay their own fare and come here as free labor. With the growing frantic demand for cotton, what would have happened to the anti-slavery amendment?

Public demand and private profit are two irresistible forces that recognize no immovable object, and it would be a long time before McCormick could acquire enough technology to eliminate most of the manual labor in the cotton field. The end of slavery was a fond hope in the hearts of thinking Southerners, but that its end would be a fiery nightmare of slaughter was the hope of too many psychopathics.

But if the Convention delegates had refused any compromise, there would have been a split and two unions would have emerged. An important point, often overlooked, is that if there was going to be a break, this was the time to have it, before adoption of a constitution containing concessions grudgingly made, or provisions only vaguely understood, and before bitter hatreds had been built up. The two nations could have developed separately, each according to its own genius, and the door could have been left open for possible future merger. Certainly the whole world would not have come apart.

Of course, as the North gathered industrial strength, their aggressive group might have undertaken conquest of the South under some trumped up charge. Issues are always available when a nation wants to go to war. No one knows, but the whole purpose of examining the past and weighing alternative courses of action that could have been taken, is in the hope of being able to arrive at better solutions to present and future problems. At least it seems we should be able to avoid making the same mistakes over again.

CHAPTER XXX:

BEYOND THE CALL OF DUTY

So many Southern records were lost during and after the war, especially records of valiant deeds performed by individuals and more especially by the Negroes of the Confederacy. To mention that most were loyal to their native land and to their white people is a political taboo today because politicians want to paint their promises against the background of a phony past; but it is obvious that the Confederacy could not have made its brilliant record without its loyal Negroes, and no good purpose can be served by refusing to honor those who merit honors. Only a few examples come readily to hand but they show the varied kinds of service performed.

Back numbers of the Savannah Morning News contain some noteworthy accounts.[1] Thomas Williamson was servant to Captain John F. Wheaton of Wheaton's Battery, Georgia Light Artillery, and a legatee of the captain, grateful for his services. Neptune, a servant in the King family, followed Captain Low King to the war and when the Captain was killed at Fredericksburg, Neptune crossed the lines and brought back the body, a feat requiring devotion, courage and strength.[2] "Uncle" Richmond Mitchell gave some undescribed but distinguished service to the 29th Regiment, Georgia Volunteer Infantry, C.S.A.[3]

There are many verified records of Negroes regularly enlisted in Confederate units. James Clarke, a free Negro, enlisted in Company K, 28th Georgia Regiment, assigned as fifer. He served throughout the war and surrendered at High Point, N.C., and made application for pension in 1904 at age 104. He must have been 60 years of age when he enlisted.[4]

Official Records (G.S.A.) verify that Private Levi Oxendine, colored, was present for duty Oct. 1, 1861 at Camp Myers, Tenn.[5] He had been mustered in July 30, 1861 by A.B.

Hardcastle, designated as a free Negro, age 53, surely acting on his own free will. Alexander Harris and his lifelong friend, George Dwelle, entered Confederate service with the First Volunteer Regiment of Georgia, and both entered the ministry after the war.[1] Harris was known for his brave service during the Savannah yellow fever epidemic of 1876. Amos Rucker served as a fighting soldier in the 7th Georgia Regiment.[2] Moses Bentley and his brother, of Georgia, were at the Battle of Fredericksburg and helped carry the mortally wounded General Francis S. Bartow from the field. Another Georgia Negro, Richmond Elder went off to the war with Joe Elder, his young master.[3] When Joe was mortally wounded, he gave his cap to Richmond. "Keep it for me, Rich", he said; and Rich kept it for 35 years and was buried with it. Devotion? Where can you find it like that today?[4]

Tim Billing, cook for Lieutenant, later Colonel Wesley Hodges of the Columbus Guards, 2nd Georgia Battalion, performed noteworthy service throughout the war. An unnamed slave of Captain Michael Usine of the blockade runner "Marie Celeste" refused freedom because he held the position of leadsman and would not desert it.[5] "Uncle" Ben Harmon served, and was at the Battle of Jonesboro.[6] Two Negroes who had served in the war and were given places of honor in parades were Allen Griffin and Emanuel Pinks of Macon, Georgia; and Gilbert Carter of Covington must have served and served well because he was taken in by the Confederate Veterans and supported in his old age, being 100 years old in 1907.[7]

In July 1864, Confederate Navy Lieutenant Thomas Pelot carried out a surprise raid on the U.S.S. "Water Witch" in Green Island Sound. His pilot, a Negro named Moses Dallas was shot and killed in the raid, and Pelot himself lost his life; but just before taking off for the venture, Pelot ordered a young Negro out of the raiding party because of his age.[8] The boy was John H. Deveaux, later prominent in politics and founder of the Savannah Tribune. He never failed to visit Pelot's grave in Laurel Grove cemetery to honor the man he believed had saved his life.[9]

A Negro named Hunter went into battle with his master Horace Beneux in the first engagement of Captain Rief's cavalry company, Fayettesville, Ark. Acting as advance guard for General McCulloch's army in Missouri, Beneux, Hunter and two others were proceeding on foot when they were attacked by enemy horsemen, one of whom rode at Hunter and slashed him on the head and arm, then rode at Private Joe M. Scott with upraised sabre. While Scott held off his attacker with his bayonet, Hunter seized his rifle and shot the man. Some horses were brought up but the enemy opened with a four gun battery and some of the horses bolted. Hunter helped an exhausted trooper up behind Scott, mounted his own horse and pulled his master up behind him, then put into operation that well known plan of getting out of there.[1]

Col. Chilton, C.S.A. used to tell his son about being with a small force one night when a Yankee raid surprised them. He was wounded and left for dead, but his body servant escaped and hid in the dark until the enemy had left, then returned and carried his master away on his back. He got a buggy somehow and got Col. Chilton to where he could be cared for properly. Years later an old Negro applied for a pension, mentioning service with Col. Chilton. The colonel's son was asked to interview him. Hearing the same stories his father had told him many times, the son said, "I am glad to recommend you, but why did you wait so long?" "Why!" the old man said in surprise, "I didn't need no pension! I was able to make a living, but I broke my leg a while ago and can't work any more".[2]

In Marietta, Georgia, the name Bill Yopp leads all the others in the Confederate Cemetery. He and his master, Capt. Thomas Yopp, went through the war together. Afterward, when Bill had been porter to the president of the Delaware and Hudson Railroad for twenty years, he heard that his old master had lost his property and was in the Confederate Soldiers' Home. Bill went back and joined him there where

he earned the nickname of "Ten Cent Bill" because he whee-
dled dimes from everyone he met and used the money to buy
Christmas gifts for other inmates of the home.[3]

Colorful Dick Poplar had been a caterer at the Bollingbroke
Hotel in Petersburg, Virginia and his cornmeal creations
were said to be unequalled. He served as cook for some
Confederate troops and was taken prisoner at Gettysburg.
He was sent to Point Lookout Prison where the Negro
guards put every possible pressure on him to take the oath
of allegiance, but Dick treated them with cold contempt. He
declared himself "a Jeff Davis man" and didn't care who
heard him say so. He helped other prisoners by selling his
famous corn pones and endured twenty months of life in
this, one of the three worst prisons of the war. A word, at
any time would have set him free but he disdained to compromise his principles. He returned to Petersburg after the
war, became a celebrated local figure and prospered.[1]

Recently the minutes of Walthall Camp No. 25 U.C.V.
Meridian, Miss. came to light, showing that Moses Pringle,
a Negro, had served in Co. A, 24th Miss. Reg't. as bodyguard
to Frank Pringle. Mose paid his own dues, attended meet-
ings regularly and as late as 1929 his transportation was
paid for him by the camp to a reunion. His service must
have been outstanding to deserve this 60 years after the
war, but the routine manner of its recording indicates that
his case was not unusual.

Tom Strother won the affection and acclaim of Gen. Richard
Taylor for outstanding performance all during the war.
Tom's uncle had served Gen. Zachary Taylor, Richard's father, in the Indian and Mexican Wars, and Tom had served
his uncle as aide-de-camp. Tom was described by Gen.
Richard as tall, black as ebony and powerful, able to light a
fire under the most unfavorable conditions and make the
best coffee out of the most unpromising ingredients. He
could put together the best stews and roasts under battle
conditions. He took care of the general's horses and his
own, the uniforms and personal equipment, foraged for food

for the general, himself and the horses. What he did with his spare time, the general didn't say, but he remarked that he was never behind in his duties.

One night general Stonewall Jackson was holding council of war in General Taylor's tent when Tom entered with a pot of steaming coffee. Jackson rose and shook his hand warmly to the astonishment of all including Tom himself. Later Jackson explained this unusual gesture of a general to a soldier. During the battle a few days before, he had come upon Tom in an exposed position and had told him to get to a safer place; but Tom had said that Gen. Taylor had posted him there and "he'll know where to find me", and with General Jackson's permission he would stay right there. Besides, the shells weren't bothering him any.

Later in the war General Taylor had a stroke, either caused by or cured by Tom's peculiar brand of coffee. He recovered and was transferred to the Louisiana area and was there when the war ended. Tom rejoined his family there and was well and prosperous in 1879 when Taylor died.[1]

A popular army saying was that Jackson marched at dawn unless he started the day before; but whenever he marched, somebody had his horse saddled, his uniform and accoutrements ready and his breakfast cooked. This was always the unfailing task of his orderly and cook Jim Lewis. In all Jackson's furious marching and counter-marching, advancing, retreating and fighting, weary men straggled and collapsed, supply wagons lagged and bogged down, but the ammunition wagons and Jim Lewis were always up front with the general.

Jim Lewis was said to have been a slave who had refused the freedom Jackson offered him, but he may have been a free Negro. He was one of the magicians, of whom there were many, on Jackson's staff, and stood out among them superb in his own field. Jim worshipped Jackson and was inconsolable when he was killed. He was given the honor of leading Jackson's riderless horse. "Little Sorrel", in the

Richmond funeral procession. Any individual of any rank in the Confederacy, yes and many in the Northern army would have deemed it the highest of honors to lead that horse up Broad Street that day.

Jim carried on in the war with Jackson's chief staff officer, Sandie Pendleton, and when Sandie was killed, it was Jim who carried the news to the Pendleton family in Stanton.[1]

There was at least one other Negro on Jackson's staff, Jeff Shields, whose photograph is on display at Jackson's home in Lexington. His steady gaze and bushy white whiskers and his chest full of medals stamp him as a man of integrity, but little else is known about him.

Captain Dinkins recalls some incidents of Negro loyalty above and beyond the call of duty. When he said good-bye to his badly wounded friend, Kit Gilmer on the field of Sharpsburg he never expected to see him again, but after crossing the swollen Potomac and covering the tortuous 40 miles of the retreat to Winchester, he found Gilmer there ahead of him. Gilmer's man Isaac had "borrowed" a horse from a Maryland farmer and, in some way known only to himself, got his master back "where dem Yankees cain't git Marse Kit".[2]

Captain Dinkins also records the experience of Dr. W.S. Christian, colonel of the 51st Virginia, captured at Gettysburg and sent to Johnson's Island P.O.W. camp for officers. There were 13 Confederate officers there with their Negro servants. *The law allowed prisoners to keep their personal property and recognized slaves as "contraband" property.) The Negroes were not prisoners, had no rights, were issued no rations, and were under constant pressure to leave but would not. The officers purchased extra fare from the sutler's shack for them but when it became clear that the Negroes would not desert the commander closed the shack down. The winter of 1863/4 was a dreadful one in Ohio and the Officers had only their meagre rations to divide with their servants, but they all stayed. Special pressure was put on George, servant of Col. I.G.W. Steadman of Alabama. He was repeatedly interviewed and offered freedom, good clothes, work at $2 a day (excellent pay then) and a good place to live, and as an alternative, no better fate than to starve to death with his master.

"And what did you say then to Major Pearson?" he was asked. George replied, "I said, 'Sir, what you want me to do is desert, and I ain't no deserter. Down South, deserters disgrace their families and I am never going to do that.'"
"And what did the major say to that, George?"[1]
"He said, 'Git out of here you damn fool nigger and rot in prison'".

Southern Negroes participated in the tragic affair at Griswoldsville, a battle that never got into the history books. After burning Atlanta, Sherman sent two full army corps toward Macon where the only force that could be mustered against them was a make-shift army of hastily assembled militia and poorly coordinated units of old men and under age boys who formed up at Griswoldville and with not even a fence for protection, charged across 800 yards of open field against the fire of repeating rifles and cannon. Northern officers, inspecting the field after the "battle", were horrified to find the bodies of feeble old men and "little boys not over fourteen". One youngster with an arm and leg broken lay near the bodies of two brothers, his father and an uncle. "They knew nothing of fighting", said Col. Wills, "And their officers knew as little".

He noted with surprise that there were a number of Africans among the captured, who had been fighting along with white companions and had been taken in a ravine from which a heavy return fire had poured into Northern ranks at 50 to 100 yards range.

Ten years before, at Balaklava, in a similar monstrous blunder made magnificent by plumed helmets, polished breast plates, flashing sabres and neighing steeds, men made a charge that has been every cavalryman's dream of glory since. Four hundred dashing young men in their glittering armor lay on the floor of the famous "Valley of Death" after that celebrated charge. At Griswoldsville, six hundred and fourteen old men in one-gallus britches and ragged kids with dirty faces lay in the weeds of a forgotten field after seven futile charges against an impossible objective. It seems to make a difference what you wear when you make an enormous military blunder.[1]

Toney climbed up behind 19 year old James B. Isbell and refused to get down and go back to the house, so they both finally rode off from Sumter County, Alabama, and joined General Forrest's free swinging cavalry. Forrest hit hard and often but Toney and James were with him all the way, including the disaster at Franklin. Captain James Isbell surrendered at Gainesville May 9, 1865 with Toney by his side.

In 1914, young Frank Isbell, age 15, was sent to Idabel, Oklahoma to teach an Indian how to mange a Ford car purchased from Frank's uncle. An old Negro with white hair and beard happened to pass and saw Frank sitting at the wheel of the car parked by the side of a road. The old man's keen eyes snapped back for a second look. "What's your name, young man?" "Frank Isbell. Why?" "I knowed it! Cap'm Isbell's grandson! Lawdy mercy! I'm your FOLKS!" Old Toney forced young Frank to go home with him for some real Southern cooking, and for a long rerun of the old stories he had heard often from his grandfather.[2]

The Tennessee Archives list 279 pension applications from colored soldiers of the Confederacy. E.H. Rennolds, in his "History of Henry County Commands" lists 26 Negroes who served with their masters, and recounts some of the services performed in line of duty and beyond. He published photos of five taken later in life. They looked like men of solid character, men one would instinctively trust.

All people in the South fought the war, either as members of the armed forces or just as civilians employing their own devices. Some showed genuine inspiration, as did a young slave of the Swetman family in Mississippi. A detail of Yankees had captured an alleged Confederate spy and were preparing to hang him. The slave boy quickly took in the situation and went into a song and dance act that so completely absorbed the attention of the Yankees that the spy was able to slip away, and was never recaptured.[1]

The Negroes of the Coney family showed organizational ability as well as ingenuity. After New Orleans fell, the plantation was the frequent victim of cavalry raids supposedly in search of war material but actually for plunder. The Negroes assumed responsibility for defense measures, and set up an early warning system. A boy with a mule would be posted at each crossroads, and at the sight of approaching horsemen would come galloping in shouting, "Damyankees! Damyankees a-comin! Pour the milk down the well!" another boy would ride for the "home guard" of boys, old men, disabled veterans and free Negro volunteers. The hams and food supplies would be hidden and the horses and live stock driven into the thickets.

The girls of the family would hang silver ware and other small articles of value to the hoops inside their hoop skirts. Jodie, aged 18 was assigned the big silver punch bowl which required an ample skirt as well as a special technique. There was never much time but the girls were always sitting demurely in the parlor by the time the raiders clattered up. Leaving the outbouildings and grounds to the enlisted personnel, the officers would search the house, which was where most valuables were to be found. When the hoopskirt hideaway became a general practice at all plantations, the raiders caught on.

The officers would manouver the girls around, and if they heard a tell-tale tinkle, would make threats. (Somehow Jodie always managed to remain seated among her voluminous folds.) The girls would weep and plead, to gain time, but often had to surrender some of the silver ware, highly prized by all plunderers.

Outside, the Negroes would greet their "liberators" with broad grins of welcome and show a laudable spirit of helpfulness; but somehow they bungled things, caused accidents, became bewildered and misdirected the searchers. The patrols, always impatient and nervous in expectation of a volley from a fringe of trees, often left empty handed, cursing the "dumb niggers" for fouling up their operation.[1]

Some of the simple services were truly heroic. When Captain Josiah Silas Wilson of Collin County, Texas, rode away with the 11th Texas mounted infantry, he took his sons and able bodied Negroes with him, leaving his wife, daughters and female slaves in the care of an old Negro man. When the captain was wounded at Pea Ridge, his wife and the old Negro took a wagon through the dangerous Indian Territory to northwest Arkansas and brought the wounded captain home, nursed him back to health and sent him off to war again. When later he came down with the fevers in northwest Louisiana, they went out again and brought him back for another cure. At the war's end, the captain returned with his sons and all the slaves that had gone away with him.[2]

"Uncle Billy" belonged to Micajah Davis of Bedford County, Virginia who was Collector of Customs for the Confederate government and had to flee with his official records when Gen. Hunter raided the defenseless Valley. The family treasures had to be elft with "Uncle Billy". After the fighting was over, Davis returned to recover the valuables. Uncle Billy went outside, tied a string between two trees and another string between two other trees. Underneath where the strings crossed, he dug up the chest of valuables intact. Not surprisingly, none of the Judge's other slaves deserted him either.[3]

Sam Russell had been purchased by the widow Russell of Searcy, Ark., in 1845. For his loyalty to the white folks, Sam was seized by federal troops and taken as a prisoner to a camp down the Little Red River. He escaped from there and made his way back with the aid of some neighbors who smuggled him through the guards. Yankees were still roaming the area so he hid out in the woods where white friends brought him food and cared for him until it was safe for him to return to the Russell home. He remained there until his death at age 97. He was buried among his white friends.[1]

A raiding party from Sherman's army on its way north came to the home of Robert Hemphill, a wealthy South Carolina planter. In the absence of all white men, they were met by a trusted old Negro, Burrell Hemphill. When the faithful slave refused to reveal the hiding place of the family valuables, the raiders dragged him at the end of a rope into the forest, hanged him and riddled his body with bullets. His 12 year old grandson witnessed the whole proceedings. A granite marker now stands on the grounds of the Hopewell Associated Reformed Presbyterian Church three miles northeast of Blackstock, So. Car. It is engraved: IN MEMORY OF BURRELL HEMPHILL KILLED BY UNION SOLDIERS FEB. 1865. ALTHOUGH A SLAVE HE GAVE HIS LIFE RATHER THAN BETRAY A TRUST. HE WAS A MEMBER OF HOPEWELL.[2]

There is another monument to faithful slaves in South Carolina, at Fort Mill, erected by two ex-Confederate officers, John McKee Spratt and Samuel White. It bears the inscriptions: DEDICATED TO THE FAITHFUL SLAVES, WHO LOYAL TO A SACRED TRUST, TOILED FOR THE SUPPORT OF THE ARMY, WITH MATCHLESS DEVOTION AND WITH STERLING FIDELITY GUARDED OUR DEFENSELESS HOMES, WOMEN AND CHILDREN, DURING THE STRUGGLE FOR THE PRINCIPLES OF OUR CONFEDERATE STATES OF AMERICA. 1865. On another facing of the monument this inscription appears: ERECTED BY SAMUEL WHITE, IN GRATEFUL MEMORY OF EARLIER DAYS WITH APPROVAL OF THE JEFFERSON DAVIS MEMORIAL ASSOCIATION, under the date of 1895. Listed as AMONG THE FAITHFUL were the names of ten slaves:

NELSON WHITE, SANDY WHITE, WARREN WHITE, SILAS WHITE, HANDY WHITE, ANTHONY WHITE, JIM WHITE, HENRY WHITE, NATHAN SPRINGS, SOLOMON SPRATT.

Alex Street was a lifelong friend of Captain Claiborne Rice Mason and a member of Mason's fabulous Negro crew that created magic bridges for Stonewall Jackson's lightning maneuvers. Mason was a self taught engineer. He had left home at the age of 8 and had made his own way in the world, impossible as that may seem. He built railroads until the war, bridges during the war, and railroads and bridges after the war. He founded the engineering firm that created such giant structures as the George Washington Bridge across the Hudson River. Alex was with him all the way, and when Mason died in 1886, it was old Alex who pronounced his epitaph. "They don't make men like Cap'm. Mason no more", he said, "The Lawd takes the same material and makes five, maybe ten men out'a it".[1]

ACKNOWLEDGEMENTS

Many thanks to those who helped: Mrs. Charles C. Alexander, Columbia, Tenn; A.B. Banowski, Houston, Tex; S.A. Bell, Roanoke, Va; H.C. Blackerby, Baltimore, Md; Mr. & Mrs. John S. Board, Culpeper, Va; Dean Boggs, Jacksonville, Fla; William M. Burdette, Jr., Salisbury, Md; Charles V. Butler, Waldorf, Md; W.E. Bradford, Irving, Tex; Edwin Lee Chaney, Searcy, Ark; Dan Cott, Meridian, Miss; J.J. Cowan, Maryville, Tenn; Wilson W. Crook, Jr., Dallas, Tex; E. Thomas Crowson, Rock Hill, S.C; William F. Cummins, Brinson, Ga; Bernard E. eble, New Orleans, La; Harrison Ethridge, Petersburg, Va; A.B. Fisher, Bowie, Md; Dr. John B. Floyd, Lexington, Ky; Bruce Fraser, Little Rock, Ark; J.L. German, Indianapolis, Ind; J.M. Grove, Fairfax, Va; Lindsay H. Gudridge, Jacksonville, Fla; Gordon Gunter, Ocean Springs, Miss; Mrs. T.O. Gurley, Jonesboro, Ga; D.H. Hayes, Houston, Tex; Gary H. Higginbotham, Biloxi, Miss; Mr. & Mrs. Arthur Horton, Grand Prairie, Tex; Scott F. Hutchinson, Richmond, Va; Fletcher F. Isbell, Arlington, Va; Frank T. Isbell, Monroe, La; Hugh B. Johnston, Wilson, M.C; Barney Philip Jones, Orlando, Fla; Marshall S. Knudsen, Marion, Ala; Allan Maul, Longmont, Colo; Donald Metz, Dape Coral, Fla; John Anderson Morrow, Clinton, S.C; Dr. Clyde E. Noble, Athens, Ga; Dr. Charles T. Pace, Greenville, N.C; Tillman C. Paschal, Puryear, Tenn; Col. David Quinn, Gaffney, S.C; Greer Raulston, Jonesboro, Ga; E. Respass Lithonia, Ga; Mac H. Robards, Greencastle, Ind; John A. Robinson, Houston, Tex; Melvin M. Sance, Jr., San Antonia, Tex; William C. Scott, Jr., Florence, Ala; Gordon B. Smith, Savannah, Ga; Col. Richard B. Smith, Kents Store, Va; Patrick Snow, Roanoke, Va; Eugene M. Stephens, Hampton, Va; Glen L. Swetman, Biloxi, Miss; L.D. Thompson, Paris, Tenn; Jack H. Watson, Tyler, Tex; Reginald C. White, Charleston, W.Va; E.A. Wyatt, Petersburg, Va; Noble Wyatt, Alton, Ill; and, of course, my wife.

REFERENCES

Page

1   1 Cridlin, Chap. III
2   2 Wertenbaker, Patricians and Plebeians, p.7
2   1 Cridlin, Chap. III
3   1 Wertenbaker, Planters of Colonial Virginia
6   1 Sir William Berkeley said that in earlier times "not one in five" survived the first year.
8   See Mannix
9 1 & 2 Northampton County records, grant of 250 acres to Anthony Johnson, Negro, for transportation of 5 colonists; see also Johnson vs. Parker, Accomac County, 1654.
13 1 All figures from Wertenbaker
14 1 One authority calculates that 13% fewer slaves were delivered to the Americas than were embarked from Africa, providing some indication of the mortality rate in transportation. Among crew members the rate was much higher, and worse yet among whites stationed along the African slave coasts.
15   Wertenbaker, P. of C.Va.
18 1 Those who tried to put an end to slavery still had no solution to the problem of how to raise tobacco and cotton in quantity.
18 2 See Washburn
19 1 See Mannix
19 2 Ibid
20 1 While almost all Virginia's manpower was up north with Gen. Washington, George Rogers Clark recruited what men were left and, on orders from Gov. Patrick Henry, led an expedition over the mountains and through the forests and swamps to the west, and secured the so-called Northwest Territory, an area that would later be divided into six states. By being in actual possession, Virginia was able to have

this area ceded to her by the treaty of 1783. Clark's expedition left Virginia defenseless against the raids of Tarleton and Simcoe, but it was a calculated risk and it paid off. The area had been declared by the king a part of Canada in the 1760's, and still would be had it not been for Clark.

23 <u>1</u> See Mannix and Conneau for good material on the international slave trade. Conneau's book is a first hand account.

23 <u>2</u> See Coon for physical features of races.

28 <u>1</u> Conneau, pp.88-89, discusses in detail the selection and treatment of slaves by ship captains and makes the middle passage appear somewhat different from popular notions of it. Mannix gives the 1786 landed cost of a slave as #27.5s.10d, and the sale price in the West Indies as #40.8s.6 1/4d, a gross profit of 39%; but reporting testimony taken by Parliament, he states that from 1680 to 1688, 249 Royal African Co. slavers embarked 60,783 slaves in Africa of whom 46,396 survived to reach their destination, a loss of 23.7%. If these percentages and prices held throughout, the slaver's profit would be about 15%, hardly enough, considering the risks.

29 <u>1</u> See Gardiner. Chaucer served in the English army against the French, was captured and ransomed by King Edward III for #16. At the same time, the king paid #20 for a horse. Prof. Lounsbury commented that the average man never brought the price of a good horse, although the #16 may have been a down payment only. (Let's hope so; after all, Chaucer was not an average man.) But Lounsbury was wrong. During his lifetime, good horses could be had for #300 or less, while a good slave might bring #1,000 or even #2,000.

29 <u>2</u> See Mannix, p.162

33   Andrews, p.421

37 <u>1</u> It is remarkable how well some slaves were pro-

vided for in ante-bellum wills, and incidents were by no means uncommon. John Laymaster, Berkeley County, Va. (Will Book 8, p.61, 1825) took care of his slaves before his family. Item 1 desired that "Andrew and Kisia" have during their natural lives land in Morgan County for a house and the executor to furnish planks, nails and timber, and after their deaths the land to be sold and the money divided among his children; but if Andrew and Kisia refuse the provisions made for them, the executor to place them "in the hands of some Christian person" who would treat them with humanity and keep them from suffering, etc. They were not to be sold on any account whatever.

37   <u>2</u> At one time, Lincoln suggested as a trial balloon that the government purchase all slaves at $300 each and set them free. This was pooh-poohed as entirely too expensive; but if ALL the states could not afford to bear the cost of freeing the slaves, how could only one-third of the states afford it?

39   A Northern mill owner had no investment in his mill hands. If they starved, became ill, left his employ or died, he suffered no direct financial loss. He could lay them off at will. Industrial employers of free labor tended to avoid contact with employees. (Perhaps some didn't want to know what working conditions were.) But some did know. How many families of the owners knew the families of the mill hands? A cold aloofness has almost universally existed.

To the slave owner, the welfare of his "people" was of vital financial interest. He and usually his family was in daily contact with workers and their families. "Massa" listened to requests, suggestions and complaints, arbitrated personal disputes, advised them in their problems, visited them when they were sick, and directed them in their work, often joining with them when short handed. This unique relationship existed on a wide scale and when put to test by a destructive war, the relationship proved itself.

39   Andrews, p.467

41   Ibid

42   1   See Mannix, p.160

42   2   See Curtin, pp.74-75, also tables 67 and 68 for ration.

48   Gov. Al Smith of New York

49   See Mannix, pp.166-167

54   Andrews, pp.330-336

56   Sellers points out that the average white per capita wealth in Alabama was $1,500, more than twice that of free America which was $711. There were 1185 large plantations in Alabama in 1860, of which Jeremiah H. Brown's nearly 9,000 acres with 4,000 of them improved, may have been more or less typical. Brown, a lawyer-planter from South Carolina, owned 540 slaves, 7 horses, 140 mules, 60 milk cows, 16 oxen, 169 other cattle and 80 hogs; raised 17,000 bushels of corn, 400 bu. oats, 1,250 bales of cotton, gave $1,500 yearly to missions and paid tuition at Howard College for 40 young men preparing for the Baptist ministry. When war broke out, he equipped and provisioned more than a regiment of Confederate soldiers. After emancipation, many of his slaves stayed with him.

61   1   See Sellers

61   2   Columbia Historical Society Bulletin. The purchase by the federal government of 3,000 slaves in the District of Columbia averaged $312 each for old and young. Most were personal servants not performing any essential services for the economy although a few were held at $2,000 each. Based on this, a figure of $500 each seems a reasonable estimate for the four million slaves in the Southern states in 1860.

68   1   Washington Star, 15 Apr. 1977

69 2 Andrews, p.467/8

70   Sandburg, Vol.2, p.155; Lincoln bought the Staats Anzeiger Newspaper, Springfield, Ill.

73 1 Timing, in politics, is vital. Lincoln's "House Divided" speech was delivered 16 Jun. 1858. Seward's "Irrepressible Conflict" speech followed in October, same year. Then, on the day John Brown was hanged, 2 Dec. 1859, Lincoln said, "We cannot object, though ppagreed with us that slavery was wrong", but if "you" try to destroy the Union unlawfully it will be "our" duty to deal with "you" as John Brown has been dealt with. Did he mean to hang ALL the people in the Southern states? But note the use of "you", "our" and "we". In Lincoln's mind, two years before secession, the split was complete, with nothing remaining but war. In less than three months Lincoln made his Cooper Union speech in New York 27 Feb. 1860, with its ringing "Right makes Might!" and the punch line, "Do our duty as we understand it". Destroy the South? What else could those words have meant? This was a step by step build-up for war, certainly not any effort to ease the tensions.

73   ppIn 1848, Jefferson Davis said in the Senate, "If folly and fanaticism" bring about a separation of the two sections of the country, "may no wounds be inflicted that time may not heal". When war did come, Davis tried to fight a defensive war. It was strategically unsound but he did it to prove to the world that the South had no aggressive intentions (as if the world cared). Despite this, Lincoln implied in his Gettysburg address that the Confederacy was not only trying to destroy the Union but the entire British Commonwealth of nations. What else did he mean by "testing whether this or any nation so conceived and so dedicated" could long endure? Would "government of the people, by the people and for the people"

(a 400 year old phrase) have "perished from the earth" if the South had won its independence? Summed up and weighed in the balance of common sense, Lincoln's lofty phrases mean nothing. Whose fathers, for instance, brought forth a new nation? Not his. History has no record of what Tom Lincoln was doing while the fathers of the Confederate leaders were winning independence and shaping the Union. Remember that in the Northwest Territory, Virginia won an undisputed title to an empire which she voluntarily ceded to all the colonies to form the Union. No other colony made such a sacrifice.

74 1 See Stern, pp.20-21. A contemporary drawing shows a Negro helping to serve the guns of the shore battery firing on the "Star of the West", suggesting that a Negro may have had a hand in firing the first shot.

75 2 The Confederate Battle Flag is not the "Stars and Bars". The Battle Flag was designed by Gen. Beauregard after the "Stars and Bars" had been mistaken for the "Stars and Stripes" (and vice versa) during the Battle of First Manassas. It is artistically the most beautiful of all flags in its simplicity, and it is the most deeply symbolical. Those are not bars one sees on the Battle Flag but the arms of a Saint Andrews Cross, all four of equal length. The cross is not standing erect as it did on the hill of Golgotha but resting on two of its arms to form the character "X", not our letter "X" but the Greek letter "Chi", the initial letter of Christ and often used for the Name, as in "Xmas". Whether or not this symbolism was in the minds of those who never feared to carry it high in battle, something shed a glory about that banner that inspired its followers to deeds of valor in the cause for which it stood.

76 1 Andrews, p.470. Garrison said that now "the compact with hell is broken".

76   2 McPherson, p.12 quotes Frederick Douglass: "I am for dissolution, decidedly for dissolution".

77   1 They all had a hand in both, of course. It was Washington's determination that pushed it through to a conclusion, and Madison's diplomacy that resolved differences and brought about agreements. Jefferson had a hand in writing it but it was Mason's Bill of Rights that was finally adopted.

77   2 Andrews, p.480. If Lincoln, instead of concerning himself so much with legalistic arguments against secession, had addressed himself to the real problem of WHY the Southern states felt impelled to secede, he might have avoided the rupture. He could have given assurance that he would work for reasonable tariffs and for guarantees of immunity from future legislative oppression. He could almost certainly have prevented Virginia and the other three states from following the first seven out of the Union, and it is likely that Virginia could have brought the seven back into the fold; but such a course would have required that he repudiate the high tariff clique and those who feared that an independent South, under a free trade policy, would build up the ports of Charleston and New Orleans and take profitable traffic away from New York and other Northern ports. And so, while the seceded states were writing free trade commitments for their government at Montgomery, the federal congress in Washington was passing bills to increase tariffs far beyond what they had ever been. What more was needed to show that the North had no intention of compromising? No effort in the North touched on the real issues, to show that Southern states within the Union would not be overwhelmed by Northern voting power (as indeed they still are).

78   1 Swanberg's book gives an excellent account of events leading up to the attack on Ft. Sumter.

78   2   If Lincoln had been sincere in his theory that a state
could not secede, and that South Carolina was still
in the Union, here was his chance to show it with a
note to the governor that observed customary courtesies and formalities. There was no reason for Lincoln to insult Pickens as he did except as a deliberate effort to provoke war. A few years later Bismark
would use the same kind of device to provoke war
with France.

78   3   See Swanberg.

81   See Swanberg, pp.236-237. Postmaster General
Blair was the only cabinet member clearly in favor
of relieving Ft. Sumter. Chase, of the Treasury,
hedged. Seward, of State, was strongly against
sending a relief expedition, and the others, Welles,
Navy; Cameron, War; Smith, Interior; and Bates,
Attorney General, agreed with Seward.

82   The vote for secession would have shown anybody
who wanted to look that it was not just a few slaveholders who wanted out; and certainly Lincoln, the
politician, would have studied the voting results
carefully. Nowhere was the voting close. Alabama's
legislature voted 61 to 39 for secession, recording
the greatest proportion of "no" votes. Florida voted
62 to 7; Georgia 208 to 89; Louisiana 113 to 17;
Texas 166 to 7, followed by a popular vote of 3 to 1.
After Lincoln's call for troops, Virginia voted 88 to
55 and confirmed it with a popular vote of 4 to 1;
Arkansas 69 to 1, and Tennessee by popular vote of
2 1/4 to 1. (See World Almanac; North Carolina figures not given)

85   Jefferson Davis still receives major criticism for the
failure of the Confederacy even in the South. His
mistakes are magnified and his accomplishments
given the once-over-lightly, while quite the opposite
is done with Lincoln. It should be obvious though,
that if Davis had made as many mistakes as Lin-

coln, the Confederacy would not have survived its first year. General Scharf, a Union officer, gives Davis credit for the almost impossible task of organizing a war effort that more than once came close, very close, to victory.

85   2   The Congress, and in fact all the branches of the Confederate government are blamed for ineptness, and their mistakes are magnified, but when it is remembered how long it takes today to get simple legislation and routine appointments through our national, state and even city and county governments, and how many mistakes are still made, the accomplishments of the Confederate government seem nothing short of miraculous. In four months time from its creation out of nothing, the Confederacy was invaded by the world's most powerful nation, and yet was able to field an army that hurled back the enemy in amazing disorder.

92   See Brewer

93   Ibid

94   1   Ibid

94   2   Ibid

96   Bates condemned the West Virginia statehood deal in the strongest terms. "Conceived as a fraudulent party trick", he said, "By a few unprincipled Radicals and the prurient ambitions of a few meritless aspirants urged it, with indecent haste, into a premature birth (lest their only chance for distinction be lost forever). "He said the bill was full of the most glaring blunders, and "any revival of a sense of justice and decency among members of congress would probably defeat it", and that "delay and the scrutiny of debate might expose its absurdity", he concluded in disgust. "And so it passed in all its deformity".

103   Southern Historical Papers

104   See Brewer, pp.102-103

105   Taylor

107 <u>1</u> Bates Diary, p.393

107 <u>2</u> See Wiley, p.175

107 <u>3</u> Ibid, p.182

109   Butler accused Father Abram Joseph Ryan of refusing to perform the last rites for dying Union soldiers. The great Confederate poet-priest assured Butler that he would be glad to perform the last rites for all Union soldiers.

109   See McPherson, p.128

110   Andrews

113   See Wiley, p.309

116 <u>1</u> See Halsey

116 <u>2</u> Ibid

117   See Wiley, pp.339-340

122   See Genovese

123   See Beitzel

125   H.K. Douglass

125   This remark of Grant's is just about the greatest compliment ever paid to the Confederate soldier. Why such an uneven exchange in favor of the Union forces should be so disastrous, he doesn't explain.

133   The selection of which individuals are to be born into the world is an awesomely complex process. For example: to create Individual "X", a fourth generation descendant of Male "A" and Female "B" who lived during the 1860-1965 era, a mysterious force had to arrange an unknown number of apparently hap-hazard and obscure events so that Male A would meet and marry Female B, then select one particular cell from A's 500,000 or more individually different eggs, then bring the two together at an exact moment to create an individual we shall call "C". No other cell, no other egg in all the world could have created Individual C, and at no other moment could the same cell and the same egg have met.

But the same force had to find and bring together at
a precise moment three other pairs of individuals so
that there would be four pairs of individuals in the
next generation to be united in the same way to produce the parents of X. This can be better understood when charted: (dates are approximate)

```
Born - Marr.
1850    1870    A—B   D—E   G—H   J—K
1876    1905    C————F        I————L
1910    1930         M——————————N
1935                       X
```

Without the war, the odds against any individual in
our present population being in existence would be
such a vast array of figures that the mind would lose
itself among them.

134 See Smith, pp.334-339

137 Stevens was elected to his first term in Congress in
1849, and the Lancaster "Intelligencer" exulted, "He
is the sworn enemy of the South, elected as a champion willing and able to worry the representatives
from beyond Mason's and Dixon's line". This call to
arms was twelve years before secession, and there
were many such. Some pretended that their hatred
extended only to slaveholders, but their vituperation
created no distinctions. The image they created was
of the whole South. That so much time elapsed before the Southern states took steps to remove themselves from such hostile associates shows that there
was forbearance on the part of Southern leaders.

139 Bates declared that the trial of Lincoln's alleged assassins by a military tribunal was unlawful, "the
work of Stanton, who believes in force when he
wields it but cowers before it when others wield it".

143 See Smith, p.338

143 1 Ibid, p.339

144 2 Andrews, pp.542-543. Every Northern state holding elections on the subject of Negro suffrage during the three years following the war had refused the franchise: Kansas, Minnesota, Connecticut, Michigan by a majority of 30,000, Ohio by 50,000; and New York had refused to decide the issue.

146 Even Mr. Webster spells it "scalawag" but the word obviously means some loathsome creature with scales, that wags, one that crawls from under the rubble of war, testing the air with a forked tongue for carrion. This picturesque sobriquet was applied to Southern born "collaborators". "Carpetbaggers" were Northerners who swarmed into the South after the war to fatten on what they could find still clinging to the skeleton of the South's once rich economy. Their belongings were packed in cheap luggage made of carpet material.

150 See Fleming, pp.423 and 553

154 Ibid, p.786

161 This political deal should have shown the Southern people what could be accomplished by shrewd negotiation. They might have held and even now might still be holding a balance of voting power by not being totally committed to one political party. With judicious use of its voting strength, and a commitment to principle instead of party, the South need no longer be a second rate section of the country.

161 2 Andrews, p.635

162 Has anyone ever followed up the slaves brought from the South via the "underground railroad" to see how they fared afterward? Was the lot of free Negroes in the North an extraordinarily happy one?

163 Letter in author's possession from an on-the-scene witness. *165

172 1 Savannah Morning News, 12 Feb. 1904, p.12 col.1

172 2 Ibid, 18 Aug. 1907, p.5, col.5

172 3 Ibid, 21 Jan. 1912, p.9, col.4

172 4 Ibid, 30 Aug. 1904, p.2, col.2
172 5 John A. Robinson, Houston
173 1 Savannah Morning News, 10 Oct. 1909, p.10, col.3, also 12 Oct. 1909, p.4 col.5
173 2 Ibid, 30 Aug. 1905, p.5, col.1
173 3 Ibid, 18 Nov. 1906, p.4, cols.4 & 5
173 4 Ibid, 27 Feb. 1899, p.6, col.2
173 5 Ibid, 18 Feb. 1899, p.6, col.2
173 6 Ibid, 6 May 1900, p.18
173 7 Ibid, 15 Nov. 1906, p.12, col.6
173 8 Ibid, 10 Jan. 1909, p.12, col.2
173 9 Ibid, 27 Apr. 1901, p.10, col.4
174 1 Allan Maul, Longmont, Colo.
174 2 Gordon Gunter, Ocean Springs, Miss.
175 3 Douglas H. Davis, Austell, Ga.
175   Kelley, pp.56, 69 and 80
176   Taylor
177 1 See H.K. Douglas, also Bean
177 2 James Dinkins, Southern Historical Papers, N.O. Picayune, 13 Oct. 1907
178   Ibid
179   Morton R. McInvale, Georgia Historical Quarterly; also see Finis Farr Fawcett in "Black Champions" (Gold Medal Books 1964). He states that the father of Jack Johnson, former heavyweight champion, fought for the Confederacy and contracted rheumatism fighting to check Sherman's march in Georgia. Could he have been at Griswoldsville?
179   Fletcher Isbell, Arlington, Virginia
180   Glen L. Swetman, Biloxi, Mississippi
181 1 Col. David Quinn, Gaffney, So. Car.
181 2 Wilson R. Crook, Jr., Dallas, Texas
181 3 Dinkins, New Orleans Picayune, 14 Oct. 1907
182 1 Edwin Lee Chaney, Searcy, Arkansas
182 2 John Anderson Morrow, Clinton, So. Car.
183   See Merritt.

1 Southern Historical Papers (1907) p.97
2 Ibid
3 Clarion-Ledger, Jackson, Miss. 23 Feb. 1890

CENSUS OF 1860   CHART NO. 1

	Total Population	Total Wht. Pop.	Total Negro Pop.	Total Mulatto	Total Free
ALA	964,200	526,200	438,000	36,900	2,600
ARK	435,500	324,200	111,300	14,000	150
FLA	140,500	77,800	62,700	5,300	900
GA	1,057,300	591,600	465,700	38,900	3,500
LA	708,000	357,600	350,400	47,800	18,700
MISS	791,300	353,900	437,400	36,600	800
N.C.	992,600	631,100	361,500	44,800	30,500
S.C.	703,700	291,400	412,300	28,900	10,000
TENN	1,109,800	826,800	283,000	41,900	7,300
TEX	604,200	421,300	182,900	25,000	400
VA	1,215,300	688,300	527,000	93,500	55,500
TOT	8,722,400	5,090,200	3,632,200	413,600	130,350
DEL	112,200	90,600	21,600	2,980	19,800
KY	1,155,700	919,500	236,200	46,400	10,700
MD	687,000	515,900	171,100	25,000	90,000
MO	1,182,000	1,063,500	118,500	23,600	3,600
W.VA	381,000	359,000	22,000		2,600
TOT GR.	3,517,900	2,948,500	569,400	97,980	126,700
TOTAL	12,240,300	8,038,700	4,201,600	511,580	257,050

CENSUS OF 1860 CHART NO. 2

	Total Negro Pop.	Total Negro Slaves	Total Negro Slave	Males Free	Neg.In Fed.Serv.
ALA	438,180	435,580	217,170	1,255	4,969
ARK	111,260	111,115	56,175	70	5,526
FLA	62,680	61,745	31,350	465	1,044
GA	465,700	462,200	228,850	1,670	3,486
LA	350,370	331,730	171,980	8,280	24,052
MISS	437,400	436,630	219,280	370	17,869
N.C.	361,520	331,060	166,460	14,880	5,035
S.C.	412,320	402,410	196,570	4,550	5,462
TENN	283,020	275,570	136,370	3,540	20,133
TEX	182,920	182,570	91,190	180	47
VA	526,960	471,505	230,115	26,425	5,723
TOT	3,632,330	3,502,115	1,745,510	61,685	93,346
DEL	21,630	1,798	860	1,890	954
KY	236,170	255,483	113,012	5,100	23,703
MD	117,130	87,189	44,315	39,750	8,718
MO	118,500	114,930	57,360	1,700	8,344
W.VA	21,950	19,360	10,975	1,295	196
TOT GR.	515,380	478,760	226,522	49,735	41,915
TOTAL	4,147,710	3,980,875	1,972,032	111,420	135,261

	Total White Pop.	Total White Males	Wht.Males Age 15-50	In Fed. Serv.
ALA	526,200	270,300	105,300	2,060
ARK	324,200	175,500	81,200	6,630
FLA	77,800	41,100	19,600	1,030
GA	591,600	301,100	140,500	
LA	357,600	189,700	102,000	4,180
MISS	353,900	186,300	88,300	430
N.C.	631,100	314,300	143,900	2,520
S.C.	291,400	146,200	69,900	
TENN	826,800	422,800	200,300	24,870
TEX	421,300	228,800	112,900	1,570
VA	688,300	348,800	159,800	
TOT	5,090,200	2,624,900	1,223,700	43,290
DEL	90,600	45,940	23,270	9,060
KY	919,500	474,210	227,810	41,650
MD	515,900	256,840	129,880	30,340
MO	1,067,100	563,140	286,650	80,610
W.VA	359,000	180,000	90,000	25,600
TOT	2,952,100	1,520,130	757,610	187,260
GR.				
TOT	8,042,300	4,145,030	1,981,310	230,550

CENSUS OF 1860   CHART NO. 4

	Total Pop.	Total Wht. Pop.	Total Negro Pop.	Total Mulatto	Negroes In Serv.
CAL	380,000	323,200	4,086	1,529	
CONN	460,100	451,500	8,627	1,901	1,784
ILL	1,712,000	1,704,300	7,628	3,587	1,811
IND	1,350,400	1,339,000	11,428	5,447	1,537
IOWA	675,000	673,800	1,069	565	440
KAS	107,200	106,600	625	266	2,080
ME	628,300	627,000	1,327	634	104
MASS	1,231,100	1,221,500	9,602	3,071	2,966
MICH	749,100	736,100	6,799	3,375	1,387
MINN	172,000	169,400	259	169	104
N.H.	326,100	325,400	494	253	125
N.J.	672,000	646,700	25,318	3,453	1,185
N.Y.	3,880,700	3,831,700	49,005	7,981	4,125
OHIO	2,339,500	2,302,800	36,673	16,691	5,092
ORE	52,500	52,200	128	62	
PENN	2,906,200	2,849,200	56,949	19,142	8,612
R.I.	174,600	170,700	3,952	997	1,837
VT	315,100	314,400	709	192	120
WIS	775,900	774,700	1,171	737	165
TERR	220,200	206,500	302	103	
D.C.	75,100	60,800	14,316	5,433	3,269
TOTAL	19,203,100	18,887,500	240,467	75,588	36,743
BORD SUB	3,517,900	2,948,500	569,400	97,980	41,915
TOTAL	22,721,000	21,836,000	809,867	173,568	78,664
SOU GR	8,722,400	5,090,200	3,632,200	413,600	93,346
TOTAL	31,443,400	26,926,200	5,252,934	760,736	250,668

The Indian population totalled 39,807, distributed as follows: Cal. 17,798; Mich. 6,172; Minn. 2,369; Ore. 177; the Western Territories, 13,291. California had 34,933 Asiatics (Chinese)

	Total Wht. Pop.	Total Wht. Males	Wht.Males Age 15-50	Whites In Fed Serv.
CAL	323,200	227,019	173,795	12,500
CONN	451,500	221,858	118,014	43,100
ILL	1,704,300	898,941	462,390	205,000
IND	1,339,000	693,348	334,310	155,300
IOWA	673,800	353,900	173,100	60,400
KAS	106,600	58,806	32,921	14,400
ME	627,000	316,517	157,238	55,800
MASS	1,221,500	592,231	321,114	114,100
MICH	735,100	388,006	203,371	68,500
MINN	169,400	91,704	48,441	19,100
N.H.	325,400	159,563	80,804	26,900
N.J.	646,700	322,733	165,962	60,300
N.Y.	3,831,700	1,910,279	797,565	354,400
OHIO	2,302,800	1,171,698	573,276	246,500
ORE	52,200	31,451	18,072	1,400
PENN	2,849,200	1,427,943	701,949	262,500
R.I.	170,700	82,294	44,453	17,000
VT	314,400	158,406	78,117	26,400
WIS	774,700	406,309	198,698	72,800
TERR	206,500	129,119	85,302	13,500
D.C.	60,800	29,585	15,791	10,500
TOTAL	18,886,500	9,671,710	4,784,683	1,840,400

Border States	187,260
Southern States	43,290
Total Whites In Federal Service	2,070,950
Negroes	172,010
Grand Total In Federal Service	2,473,510

CENSUS OF 1840   CHART NO. 6

	Total Pop.	Total White Pop.	Total Negro Pop.
CONN	310,000	302,000	8,000
ILL	476,000	472,000	4,000
IND	686,000	679,000	7,000
IOWA	48,000	48,000	0
ME	502,000	500,000	2,000
MASS	738,000	729,000	9,000
MICH	212,000	211,000	1,000
N.H.	285,000	284,000	1,000
N.J.	373,000	352,000	22,000
N.Y.	2,429,000	2,379,000	50,000
OHIO	1,519,000	1,502,000	17,000
PENN	1,724,000	1,676,000	48,000
R.I.	109,000	108,000	1,000
VT	292,000	291,000	1,000
WIS	31,000	31,000	0
D.C.	34,000	24,000	10,000
TOTAL	9,768,000	9,588,000	181,000

CENSUS OF 1840   CHART NO. 7

	Total Pop.	Total Wht. Pop.	Total Neg. Pop.	Free Negroes	Slaves
ALA	591,000	335,000	256,000	2,026	253,974
ARK	98,000	77,000	20,000	460	19,500
FLA	54,000	28,000	27,000	742	26,000
GA	691,000	408,000	284,000	2,721	281,000
LA	352,000	158,000	194,000	25,467	168,500
MISS	376,000	179,000	197,000	1,357	195,500
N.C.	753,000	485,000	269,000	22,686	246,000
S.C.	594,000	259,000	335,000	7,257	327,500
TENN	829,000	641,000	189,000	5,510	183,500
VA	1,250,000	748,000	502,000	49,796	452,000
TOT	5,588,000	3,318,000	2,273,000	118,022	2,153,474
DEL	78,000	59,000	19,000	16,919	2,600
KY	780,000	590,000	190,000	7,296	182,500
MD	470,000	318,000	152,000	54,210	98,000
MO	384,000	324,000	60,000	1,567	58,500
TOT	1,712,000	1,291,000	421,000	79,992	341,600
GR TOT	7,300,000	4,609,000	2,694,000	198,014	2,495,074

CENSUS OF 1790   CHART NO. 8

	Total Pop.	Tot. White Pop.	Tot. Negro Pop.
CONN	238,000	233,000	6,000
MASS	476,000	469,000	6,000
N.H.	142,000	142,000	1,000
N.J.	184,000	170,000	14,000
N.Y.	340,000	314,000	26,000
PENN	434,000	424,000	10,000
R.I.	69,000	65,000	4,000
VT	85,000	85,000	0
TOT	1,968,000	1,902,000	67,000
GA	83,000	53,000	30,000
N.C.	394,000	288,000	106,000
S.C.	249,000	140,000	109,000
TENN	36,000	32,000	4,000
VA	748,000	442,000	308,000
TOT	1,510,000	955,000	557,000
DEL	59,000	46,000	13,000
KY	74,000	61,000	13,000
MD	320,000	209,000	111,000
TOT	453,000	316,000	137,000
TOT SOU	1,963,000	1,271,000	694,000
GR TOT	3,931,000	3,173,000	761,000

Adams, C.F. 32,108,160
Adams, J.Q. 32
Alaric 69
Alexander 69
Anderson, J.R. 91
Anderson, R. 72,76,77
Andrew n37
Austin 54
Bacon 18
Balaclava n179
Banks 107
Barstow 173
Bates 54,105,113,138,n79,n94
Battle Flag n73
Beauregard 77,n73
Beecher 39
Beneux 174
Berkeley n6
Billings 173
Bismark n76
Black Friday 59
Blair n. 79
Boone 20
Booth 136,156
Brandy Station 116
Brooks 39,67
Brown, J.H. n53
Brown, John 41,67,164,n71
Buchanan 72,73,77
Bull Run 83
Buthelezi 43
Butler 105-107,114,n106
Caesar 69
Calhoun 61,62,71
Carpetbagger 146,154,n140
Carter 173
Casor 9
Chaucer n29
Chilton 174

Chimborazo 14,90
Christian 177
Clark, G.R. 20,50,n186
Clark, James 172
Clark, W. 54
Cleburne 103
Coney 172
Constitutional Convention 51,61
Cooper Union n71
Crittenden Resolutions 139,140,
142,156
Dallas 173
Davis, J.F. 40,55,71,73,81,82,91,
135,146,158,175,182,n83
Davis, M. 81
Davis, B. 181
Delaware, Lord 1
Deveaux, 173
Dinkind 101,181,n177
Dodson 84
Douglass 74,90,107
Downing 165
Drake 3
Dunmore 110
Dwelle 173
Edward III n29
Elder 173
Emerson 67
Faneuil 29
Fawcett n179
Forrest 104,116,164
Ft. Monroe 158
Ft. Moultrie 72,73
Ft. Sumter 72,73,76,n79
Freedmen's Bur. 148,149,150-
152,154,162
Freeman 130
Garrison 39,n74
Genghis Khan 69

George III 18,68
Gilmer 177
Grant 90,124,125,153,158
Grant 90,124,125,153,158
Griswoldville 178,179
Hardcastle 172
Harmon 173
Harper's Ferry 67
Harris A. 173
Harris J.F. 165
Hawkins 3
Hawley 152,153
Hawley 152,153
Hemphill 182
Hemphill 182
Higginson 41,67
History Henry County
Commands 179
Hitler 69
Hodges n173
Holmes 66
Hopkins 39
Howe J. 103
Howe S. 41
Hunter 174
Hunter D. 181
Indentured Servants 6,7,15,
16
Isaac 177
Isbell J. 179
Jackson A. 71
Jackson T.J. 85,91,116,130,
165,176,177,183
James I 4
Jefferson 54,75
Johnson Andrew 133,136,
138-142,143,144,146,147,
148,157,158
Johnson Anthony 9
Johnson Jact n179

Johnson's Island n177
Johnston 100
Jones 85
Kezia n37
King 172
Ku Klux Klan 154,155,159
Lancaster Intelligencer n136
Lankton 25
Laymaster n37
Lee 37,100,115,125,146,165
Lewis Jim 176
Lewis Meriwether 54
Lincoln A. 42,54,56,68-80,82,83,
107-110,113,114,119,122,127-
129,134-138,140,141,143,144,
146-148,156,163,164,n37
Lincoln Mrs. 108
Lincoln T. n71
Longstreet 116
Lounsbury n29
Loyal League 146,152,154,162
Madagascar 30,48
Madison 35,52,75
Marshall 42
"Marie Celeste" 173
Mason C.R. 183
Mason G. 52,75,82
McClellan 101
McCormick 21,55,167,170
McCulloch 174
McInvale n179
Milliken's Bend 115
Morgan 3
Mudd 138
Napoleon 37,69
New Orleans Picayune n177,n178
N.Y. Tribune 153
Parker 9
Pea Ridge 181
Pearson 178
Pelot 173

Pendleton 177
Penn 39
Phillips 74
Pickens 72,76
Pinks 173
Pleasanton 116
Polk 54
Poplar 175
Port Hudson 115
Priest 40
Pringle 175
Prisoners 114,122,124
Prosser 41
Republican Party 53,58,70,
146,147,151,159,160
Rief 174
Rolfe 4,8
Russell 182
Ryan n106
Santa-Anna 54,73
Scalywag 146,154,n140
Scott Joe 174
Scott Win. 54,73
Seward 57,n71,n79
Shepherd 67
Sheridan 119
Sherman 103,119,125,183
Sherwood Forest 66,67
Shields 177
Simcoe n20
Smith n79
Smith, John 19
Spratt 182,183
Springs 183
Staats Anzeiger n68
Stanton 114,122,127,137,138,
139,157,158,195
Star of West 73,79
Stars and Bars 73
Steadman 178

Street 183 159
Strother 175,176
Stuart 116
Sulla 145
Sumner 142-145,151,157-159
Swetman 180
Tarlton n20
Taylor 104,176
Tilden 158
Tinsley 84
Toney 179
Train 43
Tredegar 91,92,94
Tubman 161
Turner 21
Tyler 67
Union League 149,152,154,162
Usine 173
Walker 42,74
Walthall 175
Washington B. 42
Washington G. 75,n20
Washington M. 66
Washington Star n67
"Water Witch" 173
Welles n79
Wheaton 172
Whig 58
Whitney 21,35
White 182,183
Wilberforce 42
"Wild Cargo" 33
William I 69
Williamson 172
Wills 178
Wilson 181
Wise 67
Yopp 174
York 19

Stevens 136,142-146,151,157- 159   Zanzibar 30,48

BIBLIOGRAPHY

Andrews, Matthew Page, Virginia, The Old Dominion, Dietz, Richmond, 1949

Bates, Edward, Diary

Bean, W.G., Stonewall's Man

Beitzel, Edwin W., Point Lookout Prison Camp, 1971

Brewer, James H., The Confederate Negro

Brooks, U.R., Butler and His Cavalry

Conn'eau, Theophilus, A Slaver's Log Book, Prentice Hall, 1976

Columbia Historical Society Bulletin

Confederate Veteran's Magazine

Coon, Carlton S., Living Races of Man, Knopf, 1965

Craven, Avery, Reconstruction, The Ending of the Civil War, Holt, 1969

Cridlin, William Broaddus, A History of Colonial Virginia, William Printing Co., 1923

Cruden, Robert T., The War That Never Ended, Prentice Hall, 1973

Curtin, Philip D., The Atlantic Slave Trade, A Census, Univ. of Wisconsin Press, 1969.

Daily Clarion Ledger, Jackson, Miss., 23 Feb. 1890.

Davis, Burke, To Appomattox, Nine April Days, Rinehart, 1959

Douglas, Henry Kyd, I Rode With Stonewall, Univ. of N.C. Press, 1940

Fishwick, Marshall, Gentlemen of Virginia, Dodd Mead, 1961

Fleming, Walter, Civil War and Reconstruction in Alabama, Univ. of California Press, 1905

Gardiner, John, Life and Times of Chaucer, Knopf 1977

Genovese, Eugene D., Roll, Jordan, Roll

Greene, Robert E., Black Defenders of America, 1775-1973, Johnson Publ. Co., 1974

Hale, Laura Virginia, Four Valiant Years, Shenandoah Publ. House, Strasburg, Va., 1973

Halsey, Ashley, Who Fired The First Shot?

Helper, Hilton Rowan, Impending Crisis, Doubleday 1966

Henry, Robert Selph, Story of the Confederacy, Bobbs Merrill, 1931

Hume, Ivor Noel, Here Lies Virginia, Knopf, 1963

Keiley, Anthony M., In Vinculis, Blalock & Co., N.Y., 1866

McColley, Robert, Slavery In Jeffersonian Virginia, Univ. of Ill
Press, 1984-1973

McDonald, Archie F., Make Me A Map Of The Valley, Southern
Methodist Univ. Press, 1973

McPherson, James M., The Negro's Civil War

Mannix, Daniel P., Black Cargoes

Merritt, Dixon, Martha's Children, Mason & Hanger 1928

Nevins, Allen, War For The Union, Scribner's, 1971

Poe, Clarence, True Tales Of The South At War, Univ. of N.C.
Press, 1961

Pollard, Edward Alfred, The Lost Cause, E.B. Treat & Co., N.Y.,
1867

Priest, The Rev. Josiah, Bible Defense Of Slavery, Pub. by Rev.
W.S. Brown, Glasgow, Ky., 1852

Rennolds, Lieut. Edwin H., A History Of Henry County Commands, Continental Books, 1961

Roark, James L., Masters Without Slaves, Norton, 1977

Sandburg, Carl, Abraham Lincoln, The War Years, 4 Vols., N.Y.,
1939

Scharf, Gen. Morris, Jefferson Davis, His Life and Times, 1922

Sellers, James B., Slavery In Alabama, Univ. of Ala. Press, 1950

Smith, Gene, High Crimes And Misdemeanors, Morrow, 1977

Stern, Philip Van Doren, The Confederate Navy, Bonanza, 1962

Swanberg, W.A., First Blood, Scribner's, 1957

Sykes, Capt. William, Biographical Sketches of Co. B., Nashville

Taylor, Gen. Richard, Destruction and Reconstruction

Washburn, Wilcomb, The Governor And The Rebel, Univ. of N.C.
Press, 1957

Wellman, Manly Wade, House Divided, 1966

Wertenbaker, Thomas J., Planters Of Colonial Virginia; also Patricians And Plebeians, Russell & Russell, 1959

Wiley, Bell Irwin, Southern Negroes

Wilson, Edmund, Patriotic Gore, Oxford, 1962

In seeking support from foreign countries, chiefly Britain and France, the South had only cotton and tobacco for bargaining purposes, plus promises of future alliances. They were not enough. The North had wheat. Although Britain and Europe badly needed cotton for their mills, wheat was their greatest need. Thanks to McCormick's Virginia Reaper, our Western states and territories were supplying the western world with food. And the odds against Southern success, in the eyes of calculating diplomats, were enormous. Pious sentiment usually manages to get itself aligned with the interests of the pocketbook and the belly.

RETALIATION FOR BROWN'S HANGING

In a TV broadcast by George Bowles of Richmond, a descendant of Dr. Hunter McGuire told of the difficulty Winchester Medical College had in securing cadavers. Students were constantly on watch for opportunities to secure a body for research and when, in 1859, some found, in a field, the body of a man who had been shot, they retrieved it for the college. It developed later that the dead man was a son of John Brown. Three years later, in 1862, Gen. Nathaniel Banks occupied Winchester and burned the college in retaliation. Was that for preservation of the Union?

NULLIFICATION

(Note, p.62) Nullification was not by any means exclusively a South Carolina doctrine. Although it was suggested by Calhoun and was the reason Andrew Jackson regretted on his death bed that he had not hanged Calhoun, the principle was actually put into effect by several Northern states during the 1850's without anyone being hanged. The laws that were nullified were the Fugitive Slave Law and Article IV of the Constitution.

CAUSE OF THE WAR

(Ref.p.131) What caused the War Between the States has been the subject of endless discussion with a wide diversity of conclusions. What the war leaders declared at the time has to be examined impartially in light of later developments. What the soldiers themselves said or thought they were fighting for means little. Each man may have been fighting for a different objective, or perhaps because it seemed the thing to do. After all, everybody else was doing it. But the efforts of all were coordinated and directed by a tight group of politicians behind the scenes, behind the generals, and behind the backs of the people. That is a necessity of war. The real purpose, and how good or bad can only be determined by later analysis. Surely, there has been enough time since 1865 to arrive at some truths about the reasons why this war was fought.

Many people are unprepared to agree that destruction of the South was the real objective of the North, but certainly that conclusion fits all the facts. The South was indeed destroyed, many of her finest lives cut off in their prime, her most influential families impoverished and scattered, much of her most valuable property burned, her storehouses emptied, horses, mules, farm stock slaughtered or confiscated, her slaves freed, farms laid wasted, her currency rendered worthless, her citizens disenfranchised, her courts, her laws, and all her government functions displaced by an alien and arbitrary military despotism. Destruction could hardly have been more complete, more deliberately systematic, more thoroughly planned. Annihilation of the white South was the declared objective of the Stevens-Sumner political group that controlled the government during and after the war. Where was any room for preservation? What efforts were ever made to preserve any part of what had been.

LINCOLN'S POPULARITY

It is cause for wonder among some that Lincoln, although enjoying only a low level of popularity as a living president, was worshipped

as a demigod upon his death, but it should not be astonishing. It is
a good example of mob psychology.

While he lived, Lincoln had few friends, not many admirers, and
no worshippers at all. Had he died a natural death, his memory
would have dried up with the public's fickle tears, but assassination always confers some degree of sainthood on its victim. With
Lincoln, however, there was the added element of fortuitous timing.

The long, uncertain war had come to a sudden end and the Northern public, all the diverse elements of it, were united in a grand
euphoria. Emotion was at its highest pitch, as high as it could get
without unpredictable results. The President, always the most visible target for praise or blame, could hardly have escaped, at that
dramatic moment, the public's lavish adulation and praise. What
the people might have done in the next few days or weeks is a matter for conjecture. Lincoln was the national hero at that moment,
and heroes are made for worshiping.

Booth's pistol exploded at that moment, a psychological moment if
there ever was one, and it froze for all time the popular image of
Lincoln at its zenith. Forever after, "de mortuis nil nisi bonum"
would be the inviolable rule.

NEW STATES

The Struggle to get new states admitted as slave states was entirely political and not at all for the purpose of spreading the principle or practice of slavery. Southerners mistakenly believed that
new states, merely by agreeing to permit slavery, would have a political bond with the old Southern states and stand with them
against the ambitions of the industrial states to dominate the
country.

On the other hand, contrary efforts to have new states admitted as
"free soil" were not motivated by any moral opposition to slavery

but were also political, social and economic as well. The political motive was the urge for national control. Socially, the people of the West did not want an incursion of Negroes; and economically, there was the fear that free labor could not compete with slave labor in the new areas opening up. People did not seem to realize then that slave labor could only be successful in raising tobacco and cotton.

HOW MANY RUNAWAYS?

Comparing population figures can reveal interesting things. In 1840, there were 180,000 Negroes in the Northern states and territories including the District of Columbia. (Although the D of C, by geographical location and popular sympathy was Southern, statistically it has to be considered part of the North) By 1860, there were 240,000 Negroes in the North, an increase of 33 1/3%. How much of this increase resulted from efforts to lure slaves away from the South?

Comparatively, in the Southern states, there were 198,000 free Negroes in 1840, and this number had increased to 257,000 by 1860, an increase of 30%. If we knew how many slaves had been manumitted during those years (and had remained in the South) we would know what the biological increase had been. Applying the same percentage to the Northern population would give us a more or less accurate estimate of the number of slaves that had sought sanctuary in the North. However, with the figures we have, it is easy to see that the number of runaways would be far from the wild claims made that the underground railroad "rescued" from 25,000 to 100,000 slaves. Southern whites increased 78% without massive immigration. Perhaps a good guess would be that 5,000 to 10,000 slaves defected over that 20 year period, but whatever the number, they were undoubtedly easily replaced and that meant more business for the slave traders.

THE WAR'S EFFECT ON GOVERNMENT

Effect of the war upon the North and upon the country as a whole, is another subject and would require another field of research. Distinction would have to be made between those things caused by the war and those brought about by the things that caused the war in the first place. Besides, there have been five wars since that time, each with effects of its own; and since the Revolutionary War, each generation has been called out to fight, but the so-called Civil War was the costliest. America was defeated in every battle and bore all losses in lives and property. Almost all property loss was borne by the South, and proportionately more lives, perhaps actually more lives because so many of her citizens, forced by post-war economic conditions, left the South and never returned.

Not much research is needed, however, to understand how our political philosophy was affected. Lincoln's refusal to curb the corruption that spread itself throughout the government, and his "greenbacks", the phony money with which he financed the war, were causes of the 1873 panic for which Grant received perhaps more than his due share of blame. Lincoln's liberties with the Constitution left the nation something less than a republic and not a democracy but an autocracy, a government with powers that it had appropriated to itself, a government dominated by a Congressional cabal responsive to certain special interests, a de-facto extra-constitutional imperial government ruling over a group of politically inferior, economically dependent states. This was exactly what the Northern industrial clique had set out to accomplish, and what George Mason had predicted.

This new form of government expanded under impetus from succeeding wars, the proliferation of special interest groups, and the development of sophisticated political techniques.

Politicians found it expedient to deal with the leaders of groups that were politically organized and could deliver votes "en bloc". Dealing consisted of agreeing to sponsor legislation of financial advantage to group members (and leaders).

The vast number of GAR veterans constituted the first really big political pressure group, demanding government jobs at all levels, Civil Service preference, and pensions. These benefits and privileges were sectional. Confederate veterans, of course, could not participate, and therefore never could be equal within the Union. All federal largesse was lavished on Northerners while the people of the South, beside being excluded, were forced to pay the major part of the expense.

Each political pressure group always expects more from the economy than it contributes to it, and when groups were few and not always visible to the non-political eye, they could get what they expected without disaster to the economy though the expense was great. Now things are different. Every individual in the country belongs to some pressure group, and as the economy has only what the individuals put into it, there is no way each group can succeed without a "gimmick".

To complicate matters, just about every individual belongs to more than one group or has family members in other groups. Consider these groups: Retired Persons, Labor Unions, Farmers, Veterans, Teachers, Government Employees, Unemployed Persons, College Students, Blacks, Hispanics and other racial and religious groups active politically. Add up the members of all these groups and you have a total many times our actual population. If each individual is interested in three groups, you have a government that is trying to support three times its total population. Or think of every one in the country with six hands each dipping into the U.S. Treasury. Any way you look at it, you see an economic debacle rapidly shaping up.

With growing pressure from their members, groups have no brakes on their eagerness for benefits at the expense of an unseen source. If they were competing among themselves for a portion of available funds, there might be hope of the system policing itself, but no group ever opposes the ambition of any other group. To do so might spark a backfire and bring about undesirable reductions. How, then has this system managed not only to survive but increase enormously from year to year? What is the "gimmick"?

The "gimmick" is the Deficit. A deficit may seem just a ghostly, unreal something that will evaporate in the sunshine of the prosperity that is always just around the corner, but a deficit is money that is not yet earned, borrowed from workers not yet born, and borrowed with intent to default. It is a self perpetuating blight upon economy and its evils cannot be avoided. Like a cancer, it cannot cure itself. It must be excised, cut out, no matter how much the patient screams.

Otherwise, federal benefits will keep increasing to meet higher prices and increased living costs while at the same time the federal benefits will keep pushing up living costs by reducing the value of money and enlarging the deficit. This financial rat race has to crash because there is no limit on price increases but a zero limit on money depreciation, and as the zero point is approached, selling of products comes to a halt. Why sell today? Prices will be higher tomorrow. A prudent worker who took out what was a substantial insurance at the time may not be leaving his widow enough to buy a cheap coffin for him. Insurance companies and banks fail because the good money they loaned is being repaid in worthless money. Starvation, no longer a rumor, is real, and people don't starve quietly. Mobs gather in the streets, and the chaos beckons to the would-be dictators who are always lurking in the wings.

In the hope of at least postponing economic collapse while still dispensing federal benefits, some politicians would divert funds from national defense to public welfare instead of borrowing against the future. They ignore two consequences. Postponement aggravates the economic problem and makes solution more difficult; and gambling with defense funds is an open invitation to foreign interests to gamble on dominating the nation. But we have the best instrument in the world for the solution of just such problems: the Budget.

The federal budget has three parts: (1) National Defense, (2) Maintenance of necessary government departments, (3) Public welfare (an entirely new government function and never dreamed of by those who founded this nation.)

Defense is first because on it depends the very existence of the others. Maintenance of the government itself must come next and public welfare can only hope for what may be left over. This makes the first question, "How much for defense?"

We must have enough defensive capability to blunt a sudden attack and enough offensive capability left to destroy the enemy's ability to keep fighting. There is no fine line between adequate and inadequate defense but we should be able to estimate how much would overwhelm an enemy effort against us. Why try to be half safe?

Too many people are clamoring for more benefits at somebody else's expense and have no room in their eagerness for reasonable consideration of anything else. Any suggested change is viewed as an attempt to deprive them of what they have come to consider as a right. But no one is suggesting terminating or even reducing benefits, only eliminating the annual increase in benefits. This would halt the upward spiral of living costs, enable money to retain its value, reduce and eventually eliminate the deficit, and with a strong defense, eliminate chance of foreign attack. All benefits would then be safe.